GREEN HOMES

DWELLINGS FOR THE 21st CENTURY

E. Ashley Rooney
With David Hartke and John C. McConnell

4880 Lower Valley Road Atglen, Pennsylvania 19310

Acknowledgments

John McConnell and David Hartke, the two illustrious contributors to the text of this book, played a major role in its creation. I also must thank my husband Peter Lund, Phil Rossington, Phil Poinelli, and Anne Cuervo, who helped me sort out my ideas. Emily Hagopian, photographer, brought the works of several architects to my attention, and Sean Neilson, photographer, contributed several novel images. Finally, Middlesex County (Massachusetts) builder Jack McHugh explained and demonstrated many of the green terms.

Copyright © 2008 by E. Ashley Rooney
Library of Congress Control Number: 2008924094

Covers and book designed by: Bruce Waters
Type set in Exotc 350 Lt.heading font/Zurich text font

ISBN: 978-0-7643-3033-9
Printed in China

Photo Credits:
Front cover: Top, left to right: courtesy of Kevin Rolly; courtesy of Daniel Afzal; courtesy of Jeff Heatley; & courtesy of Bill Sanders. Main image courtesy of www.emilyhagopian.com. **Spine:** © Prakash Patel. **Back Cover:** Top, left to right: © Philip Beaurline; Photo by Trey Hunter; courtesy of Bill Sanders; courtesy of www. emilyhagopian.com. Main image courtesy of www.emilyhagopian.com. **Inside front cover:** © Prakash Patel. **Inside back cover:** courtesy of Chuck Choi. **Title page:** courtesy of Bill Sanders. **Contents page:** courtesy of Bruce Kelley.

Schiffer Books are available at special discounts for bulk purchases for sales promotions or premiums. Special editions, including personalized covers, corporate imprints, and excerpts can be created in large quantities for special needs. For more information contact the publisher:

Published by Schiffer Publishing Ltd.
4880 Lower Valley Road
Atglen, PA 19310
Phone: (610) 593-1777; Fax: (610) 593-2002
E-mail: Info@schifferbooks. com

For the largest selection of fine reference books on this and related subjects, please visit our web site at
www. schifferbooks. com
We are always looking for people to write books on new and related subjects. If you have an idea for a book please contact us at the above address.

This book may be purchased from the publisher.
Include $5.00 for shipping.
Please try your bookstore first.
You may write for a free catalog.

In Europe, Schiffer books are distributed by
Bushwood Books
6 Marksbury Ave.
Kew Gardens
Surrey TW9 4JF England
Phone: 44 (0) 20 8392-8585; Fax: 44 (0) 20 8392-9876
E-mail: info@bushwoodbooks. co. uk
Website: www. bushwoodbooks. co. uk
Free postage in the U. K., Europe; air mail at cost.

Printed on 100% post consumer recycled paper

CONTENTS

God has lent us the earth for our life; it is a great entail. It belongs as much to those who are already written in the book of creation, as to us; and we have no right, by anything that we do nor neglect, to involve them in unnecessary penalties, or deprive them of benefits which it was in our power to bequeath. –John Ruskin

Preface

E. Ashley Rooney

When I was a little girl, I would visit my cousin's house in Vicksburg, Mississippi. It was a comfortable, pre-Civil War plantation home that had escaped being burned by the Yankees. Its high ceilings, long central hallway, broad overhanging roof, and wide shady porch encouraged long lazy afternoons in rocking chairs. We smelled the flowers, watched the birds and butterflies, and told our stories. Vicksburg, Mississippi, is hot and humid, but we never felt the need for an air conditioner in that house.

Today, despite the multitude of farmer's porches about, you rarely see anyone sitting outside. I know that there are families within those big houses, but they have become totally separate from nature. A Kaiser Family Foundation study indicates that children aged 8 to 18 spend 6.5 hours a day on television, electronic games, computers, music and other media. The house has become not just a shelter or a place to live but the entire world for many.

Originally, our homes were meant to shelter us from the environment. The local climate and natural building materials determined the way our forebears constructed them. Houses in hot dry regions, for example, were often built from stone or clay, which offered the best protection against the heat and sun. Southern homes derived significant shading from deep porch roofs. These houses were simple (think of the Native American tepee, the igloo), but they worked.

As our civilization advanced, so did our concept of our home. Suddenly, our houses have become massive, sealed and tinted structures that keep the outside out and keep us within. Moreover, they often exclude light and air, relying on electrical lighting rather than day lighting. They depend on air conditioning rather than careful siting, well-planned roof overhangs, and large sweeping fans. Their design, construction, operation, maintenance, and even removal takes enormous amounts of energy, water, and materials; generates large quantities of waste; and pollutes the air and water.

As oil, gas and electricity prices rise, homeowners, communities, industries, and the governments are becoming increasingly interested in going green. According to the International Energy Agency, even if governments adopt more rigorous policies about energy, annual global energy demand is projected to grow 37 percent above the 2004 level by 2030.

As interest in conservation and concern over rising energy costs grows, many consumers are beginning to analyze where their homes are wasting energy and how the problems can be fixed. Some are going further and building green or sustainable residences, These resource- and energy-efficient buildings use sustainable or renewable construction materials to the maximum extent practical and are designed to be healthy, comfortable, and easy-to-live-in residences that make a positive contribution to their communities.

The growing popularity of green buildings comes in the midst of a flood of renewed interest in combating climate change, reducing dependence on foreign oil, and developing alternative energy sources. By incorporating features such as energy-efficient water heaters, Energy Star appliances, and improved insulation and renewable construction materials, a residence can be considered "green" or sustainable. In broadest terms, "green" means leaving the world in which we live a better place for our children.

Let it not be for present delight nor for present use alone.
Let it be such work as our descendants will thank us for. –John Ruskin

The most widely regarded benchmark is the Leadership in Energy and Environmental Design rating system, or LEED, from the U. S. Green Building Council. By its definition, a green home uses less energy, water, and resources and creates less waste, like greenhouse gas emissions. Green design, however, is not achievable by a single straightforward methodology. It is not just green products or a new low-energy, high-performance design or the use of sustainable products. It is the thoughtful combination of these factors and many others cast into an integrated design.

The National Association of Home Builders (NAHB) and McGraw Hill Construction project that green homes will increase from 2 percent of U. S. housing starts in 2005 to between 5-10 percent by 2010. Consumers today, however, find themselves in unfamiliar territory cluttered with green products and technologies but without many reliable guideposts about what is effective. They wish to save on water, energy, and waste but understanding the many new green products and practices can be overwhelming. Even builders acknowledge that the various "green" labels or terms are confusing!

Moreover, these products and technologies can be initially expensive. Many green houses use solar power to heat the water. A solar panel runs from about $1,000 to $1,500, and a standard water heater is generally needed for backup. Some houses rely on rooftop catchment systems to collect rainwater for irrigation purposes. Although they can be as simple as an old barrel, more extensive systems run $500 to $10,000. Experts say that green features tend to add from 3 to 5 percent to the total cost of a new home, but they can save money later. Investments in some green technologies (e. g., a green roof) can provide additional comfort and have immediate payback. Although government subsidies can reduce that cost, the payback in energy savings can take several years. [1] Over the next decades, energy prices will increase, however, resulting in a shorter payback period.

Although many would insist that a green house should be small, numerous consumers are unwilling to give up those extra square feet. On the other hand, many of those same consumers tend to implement more green features in their home because they have the wherewithal to do it.

As manufacturers roll out new energy-efficient designs, products, and technologies, many states are working with utility companies to make green energy available to consumers. Your utility will have information. The Department of Energy website (www. eere. energy. gove/greenpower) contains a great deal of material on green power programs.

Designing a green home is a complex undertaking. Many factors need to be taken into account: site, sun, and water patterns; layout; building envelope; selection, use, and disposal of materials; community; appropriate technologies; and indoor environmental quality. In reviewing the residences presented here, you will see that many choices have been made. Some, such as the Big Dig House, have opted to emphasize the use of recycled materials; others have concentrated on maximizing passive strategies. Some have used cutting-edge technologies and still others have emphasized natural light, fresh air, and absence of toxic materials and off-gassing.

The residences presented here have been selected to demonstrate the range of potential solutions. Building a green house is more than energy efficiency and preservation of natural resources; it is about creating a home that integrates cost-effective design and materials to better the well being of their inhabitants

Go Green

While you are dreaming about your new home, you can start living green. Small changes can substantially reduce energy costs. Some take minimal effort, such as using motion detectors to automatically shut off lights or letting dishes air-dry in the dishwasher. Through a mix of smart appliance purchases and careful use, you can save substantially on electric, gas, and home heating bills and own a house that is healthier to live in and easier on the environment. A professional energy audit can help you identify where you can get the best return on your investment.

In the meantime, here are some things you can do at home:

1. Boost Heating Efficiency,

Energy constantly leaks in and out of homes through our doors, windows, roofs, and foundations. In the winter, when the outside temperatures are lower than indoor temperatures, heat tends to flow outwards. In the summer, the pattern is reversed.

Energy efficiency requires that the outer skin or building envelope (e. g., the walls, roof) is sufficiently insulated and air tight. Seal your air leaks, improve your insulation – especially in places like the attic and basement – and install shades or thermal shutters to cover windows at night to reduce energy

1. Carlton, Jim, "Green House Effect: Eco-Conscious Homes," In *Wall Street Journal,* 1-26-2007.

losses in the winter and heat gain in the summer.

Check your home's heating and air-conditioning (HVAC) system. Probably the largest power draw and the greatest source of energy loss as well, your HVAC system needs to be serviced regularly and the filters on your heating unit need to be changed. A dirty filter can dramatically decrease heating efficiency, yet it only costs a few dollars and takes a few minutes to replace.

Sealing your duct system is also an easy way to save energy. A leaking duct system will absorb unheated air and let it into your home. Seal the holes and gaps with duct mastic instead of duct tape. The attic and basement are common sources of drafts, so check carefully there. Small holes and cracks where air can leak appear around plumbing pipes, telephone wires, electrical outlets, exhaust fans, dryer vents, sink and bathtub drains, fireplaces, and under countertops.

2. Program Your Thermostat

Thermostat control is a matter of personal preference, but 68 degrees during the day and 55 degrees at night is recommended.

3. Upgrade Your Hot Water Heater

Hot water heaters are major energy consumers. If you have a tank-style hot water heater, wrap it with insulation, especially if it is in an unheated area of the house. If you need a new hot water tank, choose one with a 9- to 12-year warranty, with thicker insulation and more powerful burners. Tankless, on-demand hot water heaters may improve heating efficiency, since they do not have to constantly heat a large tank of water.

Consider reducing the temperature on the water heater to about 120 degrees Fahrenheit, the optimum temperature for water heating comfort and efficiency

4. Replace Decrepit Windows

Windows can be a major source of heat loss in the winter and heat gain during the summer. With windows covering so much wall space these days, do select the most energy-efficient ones you can afford. Double-pane windows are standard in new construction in most cold weather markets. Insulating features such as heat reflecting, low-E coatings, and argon gas between glass panes to slow down heat transfer make new windows very attractive. They can save you between 10 to 25 percent on your heating bill, but they are expensive for an average home.

Efficiency can be obtained by ensuring that the windows are tightly sealed. Of course, weatherstripping should always be used in the cool months to seal any open spaces that exist around windows or doors.

5. Go for That Healthy Air

A healthy home should be free of toxicants, irritants, and substances that cause allergic reactions. Eliminating harmful substances from your home is the most effective way of ensuring that your indoor air quality is healthy. To keep your air clean, choose cleaning products free of toxic chemicals, paints, and wood finishes that are natural and contain few or no volatile organic compounds (VOCs). Kitchens and bathrooms should have a quiet, reliable exhaust fan that vents outside. Some builders also install exhaust fans in garages to prevent vehicle fumes from building up.

6. Control Your Humidity

Mold growth on inside walls can occur during the heating season, especially on the surfaces nearest the outside of your home. Moisture traveling through the air from the bathroom, basement, kitchen, or other sources may condense when it comes into contact with a cold wall. By having well-insulated walls, you not only can save energy, but you also can reduce the likelihood of condensation and mold. You can raise the temperature of your walls by increasing the circulation of warm air from your heating system.

During the heating season, an indoor humidity level below 40 percent will prevent condensation in homes in most parts of the country. A lower level of humidity or extra insulation may be needed to prevent condensation in homes in very cold areas.

7. Swap Your Light Bulbs

One of the best things you can do to be more energy efficient is to replace old incandescent light bulbs with compact fluorescent bulbs (CFLs). Last year we gave each person on our gift list one of these bulbs. This year we are replacing every bulb in the house.

Energy Star qualified CFLs are required to meet certain standards, one of which is they have to save you at least $30 in energy costs over the bulb's approximately 7,500 to 10,000 hour life according to *Consumer Reports* (October 2007). Multiply that by the number of lamps and fixtures in your home and watch the savings add up. Some people also prefer light emitting diodes (LEDs), which can be more expensive but use little energy.

8. Conserve Water

Low-flow plumbing fixtures keep money from going down the drain. Dual flush toilets use less water per flush than older models; low-flow showerheads use 2.5 gallons per minute or less (conventional models use 5 to 8 gpm); and low-flow faucet aerators cut water usage to as low as 1 gallon per minute. Cisterns, which can be an old barrel, can collect rainwater to be used for watering gardens or your flowerpots.

9. Purchase Energy-Efficient Appliances

Buying energy- and water-saving appliances saves money on the electric bill and helps the environment. Check out Energy Star labels on kitchen, laundry, and bath appliances and fixtures. When purchasing energy-efficient appliances, focus first on refrigerators because they run all the time. Air conditioners also tend to use a great deal of energy. This year, the Department of Energy will be updating energy-efficiency standards for all appliances, so watch for even more efficient products to come onto the market.

Set your refrigerator temperature to 37-40 degrees. Setting the temperature 10 degrees below the recommended levels can increase energy use by 25 percent. Make sure refrigerator door gaskets seal tightly. If not, replace them.

Defrost your freezer before frost builds up to one-quarter inch — this keeps it running efficiently.

Use a vacuum cleaner or soft brush to clean the condenser coils behind or underneath your refrigerator and freezer several times a year.

Dishwashers use less water than hand washing. Run full dishwasher loads and air-dry dishes when you can, unless your home has mold or mildew problems.

Consider using a small toaster oven for baking instead of heating up a full-size oven.

10. Watch That Fireplace Flue

Close fireplace and wood stove dampers when not in use. Warm air rises right up an open chimney – just like leaving a four-foot window in your home wide open. If you can still feel a draft with the damper closed, consider installing tight-fitting fireplace doors or a fireplace draft stopper plug.

11. Reduce, Reuse, and Recycle!

Recycling saves landfill space, reduces the cost of waste disposal, and can save energy and our resources. Recycling a ton of glass saves the equivalent of nine gallons of fuel oil, for example. Reprocessing used materials to make new products and packaging reduces the consumption of natural resources. Recycling also reduces pollution risks by keeping materials out of landfills.

12. Remember Nature

Vegetation and landscaping can help keep a home warmer in the winter and cooler in the summer. Trees planted upwind from a house, for example, can create a windbreak, protecting a house from cold January winds.

Poorly drained home sites can be a major problem – from mold to structural damage. A well-landscaped site can soak up melted snow and heavy rainfall. The more water that soaks into the soil, the less runs over the surface, causing erosion and flooding. Reducing impervious surface areas such as asphalt driveways or concrete terraces can decrease surface runoff.

13. Buy Local Products

Buy more locally grown products that are manufactured nearby. Companies will use less fuel to transport them.

FOREWORD

THE GREEN REVOLUTION

John C. McConnell AIA

The Green Revolution is upon us. The twin prongs of renewed energy crises and global warming are prodding us to face the inescapable: our post-industrial consumer-driven and wasteful civilization cannot be sustained much longer. Awareness of this has begun, thankfully, to reach the level of popular culture, and one target of this awareness has become the way in which we build and inhabit buildings. The emergence over the last decade or so of guidelines for more methodically thinking about buildings and their impact on the planet have quickly raised public awareness of the issue. Virtually every architect, builder and developer now markets himself as "green." Even filmmakers and politicians have gone public with the issue — and most spectacularly winning the Nobel Peace Prize.

But we still lack a popular consensus of what "green" really means and how it applies to everyday choices made by average people. Most guidelines for increasing the "sustainability" of buildings, like the LEED (Leadership in Energy and Environmental Design) program of the U. S. Green Building Council, have tended to focus on institutional and commercial projects, while programs for evaluating houses are just beginning. In 2002, only 38 buildings received a LEED rating; by 2007, 1,326 residential and non-residential buildings earned LEED ratings. It is in the design and construction of houses that a large majority of people would most likely encounter these issues on a personal level.

In the pages that follow, you will see a great number of intriguing and innovative adaptations of "green" thinking to the creation of architecturally and environmentally satisfying houses.

What Does Green Mean?

At the outset, you will need a definition, a short list of the concerns, which are components of the green building movement. These concerns can be summarized in four parts:

1. Energy. Many now concede that the world has passed the halfway mark in our consumption of all known petroleum on the planet, and the remainder will be increasingly difficult to extract and use. As alternative forms of usable energy are developed, we move toward greater conservation of non-renewable forms of energy, particularly petroleum, and the harmful by-products of those fuels (pollution, strip-mining, etc.), We simultaneously seek sustainable ways of heating, cooling, and lighting buildings that rely on a building's relationship to natural forces, such as orientation to the passage of the sun, sheltering earth forms, and prevailing winds.

2. Building Materials. The manufacture of the materials used in construction must now be driven by several concerns. The sources of building materials – renewable plantation farming vs. old-growth forest lumber, for example – must be scrutinized. Scrutiny also focuses on the ecological responsibility of manufacturing processes for materials, as well as a future of infinite recylability, keeping those same materials from ending up in landfills.

3. Human Health. As certain component materials of buildings age or deteriorate, they may give off compounds ("off-gas") harmful to air quality and occupant health. Here the concern is for eliminating toxic building materials and construction practices so as to avoid, for example, materials containing formaldehyde, say, or uric acids.

4. Pollution. Part of the sustainability movement is directed at creating a healthy non-polluting relationship between buildings and water, air, and land. Human waste, trash, and inefficiency of material use must be replaced by recycling systems and ways of minimizing "waste," both in the building process and in the ensuing lifetime of the building.

The Way We Were

Traditional building in every part of the planet has, for many thousands of years, generated great variety in shaping building parts – floors, walls, roofs, openings – to local conditions of environment, available materials, climate, or topography. And it has done so largely in a harmonious symbiosis with nature and planetary systems. One sees traditions that have shaped buildings by using whatever is at hand combined with human ingenuity to most efficiently capture wind, for example, or solar energy, or to use daylighting instead of artificial light whenever possible. An extreme example is the igloo, developed in the Arctic to provide sustaining human habitat in the harshest of climates and with a daunting paucity of building materials – in this case little more than snow. The semispherical shape minimizes external surface in relationship to enclosed floor area and best resists forces of wind. The warmth created in the interior partially melts the walls, which then freeze into an airtight ice membrane. At the other extreme, indigenous housing types in tropical climates, and other places where it is predominately warm and humid, have architectural forms that tend to encourage ventilation. A house raised up off the earth on stilts, for example, allows air to move below the floor. Other features have been invented: double roofs, where the outer one shades the inner one and creates a space between them where air can circulate; hatchways; or light monitors at the ridge of the roof to allow hot air out as cooler air in pulled in below.

Two millennia ago, Roman houses frequently had an *atrium* at their center. This was a larger room than average, open to the sky and useful for natural ventilation. A partial roof (*compluvium*), often inward-leaning, both shaded the room's walls and collected rainwater and funneled it into a pool or catch-basin (*impluvium*) below it in the center of the atrium, which then drained into an underground cistern. Larger houses usually also had peristyles, borrowed from the Greeks. Larger than the atrium, the peristyle was a courtyard, also open to the sky with roofed aisles on all sides carried on colonnades. This was frequently planted as a peaceful interior garden, sometimes with a fountain, which cooled and sweetened the breezes.

By no means limited to Roman houses, the central atrium feature is found in many architectural traditions, particularly Latin ones. The traditional Chinese house Yin Yu Tang, now part of the Peabody Essex Museum in Salem, Massachusetts, also features a tall narrow open courtyard in the center of the house, whose roofs direct rainwater to a pair of large tanks on the ground level, useful not only as water storage basins, but for keeping live fish destined for the kitchen.

In parts of Iran and Pakistan – the city of Hyderabad is most well known – extreme heat is counteracted architecturally by the incorporation of enormous tall "air scoops," which resemble oversized chimneys, all rising toward the prevailing winds. These capture and funnel moving air down into the house and, when there is no breeze, act in reverse to provide ventilation of warm air.

In the earliest decades of the seventeenth century, English settlement along the eastern seaboard of what would become the United States, we find an interesting set of inflections, or alterations, of traditional English building forms brought about by responses to new climatic conditions. Those who built these First Period houses in the hot and humid Chesapeake Bay region solved the problem of unwanted heat from cooking fires burning all the time in the house's fireplaces by building the great chimney masses to the exterior of the end walls, thus placing three of the four sides of the fireplaces to outside air, where the heat could dissipate outside of the house. At the same time in New England, a predominantly cold climate (particularly in the seventeenth century), builders learned to cluster all the fireplaces into a great masonry mass in the middle of the house in order to conserve and radiate the heat within the interior.

The superiority of double-hung windows, in which two pieces of sash slide up and down past one another, over earlier casements, whose sash is hinged on the side and operates like doors was evident when they were introduced into architecture from Flanders in the late 1600s. Now openings of any size could be made either at the bottom of the window, to admit breezes, or at the top, to exhaust warm or stale air.

The traditional architectural role of plants, both within and outside the house, is to help cool and purify air. Deciduous trees were always valued for coolness of their shade in the leafy summer, while admitting the warmth of the sun during the leafless winter. The famous single houses in Charleston, South Carolina, are examples of an inventive architectural form married to greenery as a result of climatic forces. These houses share the traditional one-room-deep floor plans of many colonial homes throughout the English colonies in America, but these were built with their narrow ends to the street, and their gardens to the side, rather than to the front or rear. The side garden was always to the south or west so as to simultaneously face the prevailing breezes during the warm time of year, and place shade-giving trees between the house and the sun. As breezes wafted across the cool greenery, they would be funneled into the house, whose garden façade generally featured multistoried porches, called piazzas, which were both outdoor parlors and breeze-catchers for the rooms within.

In fact, by the 1840s, American houses began to sport piazzas and verandahs quite frequently for the first time in most parts of the country. These large porches not only provided outdoor living space, but also were also instrumental in a process, culminating – via the Shingle Style – in the houses of Frank Lloyd Wright, fusing a house with its natural setting and blurring the distinction between the natural and the artificial realm.

In warm and sunny places, indigenous building practices usually found a way – overhanging cornices or broad roof eaves, for example – to use architectural elements to cast shadows on lower parts of the building at the warmest parts of the day, thereby mitigating solar heat gain. In the middle of the nineteenth century, Americans built what they called Italianate houses, whose defining feature – a broad overhanging cornice carried on ornate brackets – was borrowed from the environmental features of the medieval farmhouses of Tuscany. Indeed, with the rise in the twentieth century of European Modernism, we frequently find various kinds of sunscreens present, not only acting to diminish the effects of the sun's heat on glassy buildings, but more sneakily acting as a form of ornament, which Modernism banished because it was bourgeois and not "industrial" enough. The concrete buildings of the famed Franco-Swiss architect Le Corbusier, in places as disparate as Chandigarh, in the Punjab, and Cambridge, Massachusetts, derive a great deal of architectural effect from their deeply shadowed sunscreens, which Le Corbusier called "brises-soleil" ("sun-busters").

Recent Good, Recent Bad

Everything changed with the dawning of the Industrial Revolution in the late eighteenth century. And the vast ramifications of the industrialization of building construction have brought us to the present crisis. As we have learned to ignore climatic elements of nature through petroleum-mechanized heating and cooling of buildings, so too have we learned to concoct a bewildering array of non-natural building materials and to construct an economy tolerant of great waste of resources and land.

The explosion of synthetic materials used

particularly for dwelling house construction since the Second World War, has engendered at least as many problems as it solved. The exterior walls of wood-framed houses, for example, were never completely airtight or well insulated. This resulted in a certain inefficiency of energy use because of heat loss. But the now mandated use of synthetic materials – plastic building wrap, fiberglass, or foam insulation – to make our houses perfectly airtight, has made evident some of the ways in which old-fashioned construction methods avoided problems associated with the lack of air movement: decay, mold, illness, etc. As natural building materials became scarcer – through the depletion of old-growth forests, for example – and consequently more expensive, less costly alternatives were invented and incorporated into construction practice. Engineered products such as plywood, particle board, synthetic flooring, foam rubber, rigid insulation, polyvinyl chloride (PVC) piping, siding, windows or trim, and many others, are less costly but contain substances like formaldehyde or uric acid which have been shown to be toxic, "off-gassing," harmful substances.

Moreover, the single most unsustainable act of modern building practice has been the demolition of old buildings. Not only does this erase a cultural artifact that contains a piece of collective memory, but it also involves the removal of all the energy that has been expended and banked in the original structure. Although the movement of the last 25 years or so for the adaptive reuse and renovation of existing structures is among the most positive of green acts, it is still legal and commonplace to tear down existing houses to be replaced, generally, by substantially larger ones, rather than responsibly renovating them. And all too often the new houses are exaggeratedly larger than what their occupants would ever need – the now familiar "McMansion."

The first concerted focus on making buildings more environmentally responsible (the word "green" was not initially used) occurred in the late 1960s and early 1970s. A chief focus was discovering ways of using the sun as an alternative to fossil fuels – solar power. There are two chief ways of doing this, passive and active. Active solar energy generally results in systems within a building to convert the heat or light of the sun into useful ways to control the interior environment. Generally, these involve hardware for heating water, which can then be used for domestic hot water or for warming the house, or some sort of photovoltaic cells, which convert solar radiation into electricity to be used, stored in batteries, or sold back to the local utility. Either method can occur on a small scale within individual buildings or at the much larger and more industrial scale of a "solar energy farm" – large arrays of solar collectors or photovoltaics.

Passive heating and cooling strategies rely less on hardware and more on solar orientation, cavity wall construction, earth-sheltering, grass roofs, and thermal-mass heat storage systems. The last quarter of the nineteenth century saw the invention of the double, or cavity, wall as a thermally effective device in building. In its simplest form, known as a Trombe wall, the outer wall is made of glass, and the inner, a few feet inside the glass, is made of some heat-retaining material, usually some kind of masonry. As this thick wall is exposed to the sun through the glass, its heated mass radiates warmth into the house as necessary, and the cavity can be opened to create a ventilating airflow.

Temperatures within the earth are more stable and favorable than those of the air, which fact has traditionally been exploited in building design. Natural or manmade cavities in the earth, as well as groundwater, can be used as a constant temperature medium for the exchange of heat in air or water. Many forms of primitive dwellings, such as the sod house of the American prairie frontier, were partially dug into the earth. Earth-sheltered houses, such as those by architect Malcolm Wells in the later twentieth century, take advantage of the thermally stable properties of the earth itself by being partially buried below grade, protected from the elements and rapid changes of temperature. Although earth-sheltered dwellings have yet to achieve anything resembling popularity, Wells in a 1991 article, predicting that a new "energy crisis" was imminent, enumerated the benefits of living in the earth:

> ...living wild gardens instead of asphalt overhead, rain water considerations, silence, sunlight, low fuel bills, little maintenance, slow temperature changes, freedom from vibrations, clean air; and perhaps best of all, the feeling of having done something right for the planet. [1]

The United States has recently become a predominantly suburban nation, and attention has recently begun to be brought to the exceptionally wasteful way in which we develop our suburban land. As opposed to this sprawl, traditional urban architecture emphasizes compactness and the creation of public space. Rowhouses occupy less ground area and are more environmentally sound than a series of freestanding houses, as two of the four sides are shared and therefore insulated by the adjoining structure. Twentieth century Modernism stressed a preference for freestanding sculptural buildings, an anti-urban bias that accelerated our preference for suburban rather than urban development. And we pay a double price for this: not only are we using up formerly natural or agricultural land in an exceptionally wasteful way, but we are now subjecting our cities to the same "suburbanization," as seen for example in Boston's replacing its divisive old Central Artery with a suburban and equally divisive swath of grass, trees, and open paving with the environmentally sanctified name "Greenway."

In short, we live in a philosophical climate of dominion over nature. The green movement seeks the reduction of our consumption of nature's bounty – more efficient use of energy sources, more responsible cultivation of material resources, fewer wasteful by-products left behind, and less poisoning of the world. But even this may not be good enough. American architect William McDonough, whose practice has been at the forefront of ecological responsibility, has pointed to this sort of "efficiency" as being merely "less bad." To be actually "good," he says may take more fundamental changes in the way humans carry out living and economic activity, a more fulfilling relationship with the natural world. The net result of our activity on behalf of "sustainability" may result in slowing down ecological destruction, but not stopping it. We need, he says, more positive effects, not fewer negative ones. [2]

Various Revolutions

The seeds of the green movement were sown with the flowering of the Industrial Revolution. There had really never been any such thing as a building tradition that was massively harmful or antithetical to nature, not to mention the social order, until the dawn of the nineteenth century. Until then, there had been little technological capacity to make buildings in such a way as to noticeably affect negative changes on planetary ecosystems. Until the Industrial Revolution and the burgeoning of population that it ultimately engendered, humans lived more or less by necessity within the stream of possibilities for building and securing existence afforded by nature. In the absence

1 Malcolm Wells excerpts from an article he wrote, "Being Perfectly Clear," in *Progressive Architecture*, 1991, Mar., v.72, no.3, pp 82 - 83.

2 William McDonough excerpts taken from the preface he wrote to *Big and Green: Toward Sustainable Architecture in the 21st Century*. David Gissen, ed. Princeton Architectural Press, New York, and The National Building Museum, Washington. 2002

of sophisticated energy conversion systems, the creation of advanced and synthetic building materials, and the dictates of population pressures, human building activity remained to a greater or lesser degree in harmony with natural forces. (An exception would be deforestation resulting from both agricultural and domestic practices of clearing land for fields, and using up wood for building and as fuel.)

Building materials, for many thousands of years, were limited to durable and naturally occurring sources: wood, stone, brick, terra cotta, iron, and fabric. The same can be said for the energy sources required for those buildings: wood, coal, solar heat gain, breezes, and waterfalls (to power grist or lumber mills.) For lighting, there was the sun, or fire, olive or whale oil, or candles. When it was hot or stuffy, one opened a window. One kept cool by using building parts to create shade. One collected rainwater in barrels and cisterns for drinking, washing, and irrigating.

The traditional idea of nature for millennia was that it was in one way or another "sacred" --- because deities dwelt there maybe, or beauty, or mysterious forces which could not be understood. Human life was generally in harmony with nature, of necessity, and to a great degree controlled by it. Buildings were one of the principal ways in which humans modified nature in order to secure their own survival and comfort. Buildings, to this day, provide the necessary "second skin" which mitigates the effects of those natural forces which operate directly upon our rather fragile bodies --- temperature, light, wind, sound, atmosphere, rain and humidity, and so on.

In his 1975 book, *American Architecture: The Environmental Forces That Shape It,* James Marston Fitch described our relationship to external nature as "*uterine*." "And yet," he continues, "unlike the womb, this external environment never affords optimum conditions for the development of the individual. The building wall must be visualized not as a simple barrier but rather as a selective, permeable membrane with the capacity to admit, reject and/or filter any of these environmental factors."

With the advent of the Industrial Revolution, then, came a great change. The capacity to modify and exploit natural processes was greatly expanded, and the fundamentally balanced relationship between humans and nature was substantially altered. The sudden ability to manufacture on a vast scale and to synthesize many new things from nature's bounty brought about a new view of that very nature. No longer the sanctified and somewhat mysterious sustaining force of human existence, available to all in equal amount, nature became something that now existed for the benefit and profit of mankind; a commodity, waiting to be transformed.

And, of course, it was the structure of society itself that was also transformed. The novels of Charles Dickens, for example, describe the world of the "dark, satanic mills" and the new social order of owners and workers that stand symbolically for this new commodious of nature. And yet there were other results of industrialization to be admired, exalted, and then improved upon; industrial progress improved lives, too. It helped to increase leisure time for some and give access to more domestic creature comforts, more diversions, and more devices for making life easier to live.

Few could remain neutral in the face of this new kind of life. There were as many who embraced it as those who did not. Among the negative reactions engendered by the Industrial Revolution were various forms of turning to nature as an antidote to the industrialized capitalistic city – the "Hudson River School" of painters and poets, for example, or the rise of Transcendentalism, worshipping the "divine" nature of creation as the very dwelling place of the Creator Spirit, stressing her capacity for healing. Frederick Law Olmsted finally found a career and lasting fame for himself when he brought "nature," like a weapon, directly into the city in the form of our first great urban parks, there to provide balm to those who could not afford to escape.

The net effect of this has lasted to our own day. A new revolution seems to have started, global in scope. Brought back to life by recurrent energy shockwaves, growing dismay over the tawdriness of suburban sprawl, and the substantiation of global warming, the resurgent concern for nature and natural forces embodied by the green movement surely are the latest, and perhaps most obvious, manifestation of the shifting balance between the pleasures of industrialized society and its conscience.

John C. McConnell, AIA, is a principal of the firm McConnell+Partners Architects Inc. in Boston, as well as adjunct professor of American Architectural history at Boston College since 1979. He also is a lecturer in architectural history at the Harvard Graduate School of Design and architecture lecturer-in-residence for the Museum of Fine Arts, Boston.

INTRODUCTION

YOU CAN BUILD A BEAUTIFUL GREEN HOME...
HERE'S HOW

David V. Hartke

The common perception of an environmentally friendly home connotes some seemingly contradictory ideas. On the one hand, people love the idea of being part of saving the earth's resources on a daily basis. On the other, green homes have the reputation of being designed for sustainable function rather than aesthetics. And that is where I believe the problem lies. People need to understand that they can help save resources and do so – while living in beautiful, green homes.

The unattractive and unpolished look that, up until recently, has been the conventional image in the majority of green home articles tends to stray too much from traditionally accepted architectural models. The fear that this unique type of home might erode the architectural fabric of our warm and established communities has kept some from opening their eyes to the current reality. Consequently, few homebuyers want to take the risk of building what has been thought of as a typical green home. Until more homeowners are willing to take this risk, the obvious solution is to apply green features to homes that fit within their neighborhood. The good news is that green characteristics can be implemented into the design of nearly every style of home.

The key is to start with an architectural style that works within the region or climate for which it was originally designed. For instance, an elegant Queen Anne, Victorian home with steep roof pitches that shed rain in San Francisco should not be placed in the hot arid climate of Arizona. The same is true of building a stout pueblo home in Alaska. It just doesn't work.

Climate is a major factor influencing green design. Our globe includes multiple climate systems that affect our comfort and lifestyle. Whether it is hot and humid, cold and dry or somewhere in between the two, the design of homes, prior to the implementation of heating and air conditioning systems, completely relied on working within the regional climate.

The pueblo home design, for example, was originally developed thousands of years ago in response to the local climate zone. The design concept had nothing to do with aesthetics. It was developed as a means of protecting the owner from extremely hot days and relatively cool nights without much rain. Thick solid clay, or rammed earth walls absorbed the heat during the day and released it at night, liberating the homeowners from wasting too much of their time and resources finding and cutting wood for evening heat. They also didn't need the steep roofs typical in rainy or snow-filled regions. Their home suited their climate.

There is a general misperception that only new homes can be considered green. The reality is that renovating and adding on to an existing home starts off naturally with multiple sustainable attributes. For example, existing materials can be re-used for a renovation project rather than being dumped into a landfill. Moreover, the site or property has obviously already been developed and doesn't require extensive utility work or vehicular infrastructure. In addition, the homeowner is already part of an existing community and will likely stay in his or her home for a much longer period than the standard American timeframe, which is about seven and a half years. That extended stay or lifecycle also suggests that the homeowner will be more willing to invest some additional money into more energy-efficient systems and durable materials.

It is not very hard to make your existing home considerably more energy and resource efficient. One of the simplest and most popular current green elements that the majority of homeowners have been adopting is the replacement of their traditional incandescent light bulbs to CFLs (Compact Fluorescent Lamps). The term *lamps* actually refers to light bulbs. This current changeover to CFLs provides a microcosmic vision of how the overall green movement will eventually progress.

The federal entity Energy Star states that if every household across the United States would switch one room of bulbs from typical incandescent bulbs to CFLs, these much more efficient bulbs would offset the overall energy use and pollution emission throughout the United States from 8 million cars.

The energy savings from CFLs has created its own niche market based simply on the fact that a critical mass of buyers are purchasing these new light bulbs. Corporations have now jumped on the bandwagon to gain market share. The recent competitiveness within this specific product market has already made CFLs both easier to purchase and much less expensive than they were in 2005. In addition, the technology applied by the manufacturers has modified the quality of fluorescent lamps from the original days of harsh white, flickering light to a soft and warm quality, which is also dimmable. This single aspect of the green market represents how all elements of the green housing market will progress as the corporate world catches on to the fact that consumers are moving toward sustainability within their homes.

There are many other easy-to-achieve, energy-efficient elements that homeowners can apply to their homes. The best strategy is to discern early on in the process what the focus of the home design will be: energy use, reducing the impact on the earth's resources, utilizing more durable materials, a healthier indoor environment, or all of the above. The design and construction process can employ all of those points. The key is to make sure the design professionals and contractors are all included early in the design effort.

From an indoor environmental aspect, healthy, no (or low) VOC (Volatile Organic Compound) paint, caulks, and adhesives have become nearly commonplace in the remodeling market. Everyone with any interest in avoiding indoor toxins can purchase these healthier products for nearly the same price as the traditional paints and caulks. They are readily available at your standard home improvement store. It's just a matter of reading the label and understanding that the term VOC makes a difference.

When plumbing fixtures need replacement, whether it is a toilet or simply a showerhead or faucet, high-efficiency or low-flow fixtures are also relatively easy to purchase. The standard American toilet uses 1.6 gallons per flush while a showerhead shoots out 2 gallons per minute. Today's cutting edge dual-flush toilets only use 0.8 gallons per flush. Installing simplistic aerators into faucets or showerheads can reduce their use down to 1.2 gallons per minute while still maintaining a comfortable water flow.

Homeowners that are considering major renovations have an even greater potential to save additional energy and cut their monthly operational costs considerably. If it's time for window replacement, the 'U-value" number should be your focus. An independent organization called the NFRC (National Fenestration Rating Council) tests windows for their resistance to heat loss (or gain in the winter). The lower the U-value, the better the window – with U-0.35 being a viable target. There are also other factors that help assess the quality of windows. Low-E, Argon-filled, multi-pane glass with a climate-relevant Heat Gain Coefficient Factor (HGCF) will also help save energy and money over time.

The walls the windows sit in, then become the next focus. What's great is that exterior walls can become much more efficient than the windows with minimal added expense. Insulation is the key element, and the homeowner has many choices. A high-quality CFC-free fiberglass insulation sets the baseline benchmark with systems such as blown-in cellulose, recycled blue jean, or, the most efficient of all, spray foam insulation topping the charts. The type of insulation depends on the extent of the renovation. For instance, if the wall sheathing or drywall were to be removed, spray foam would be the most efficient choice. If not, holes can be drilled into the walls and cellulose or blue-jean insulation can be blown into the wall cavity and then re-sealed. Either way, insulation makes the home much more comfortable both thermally and acoustically and provides a considerable energy and cash savings over time.

As important as the walls seem to be, the roof or ceiling should actually be the focus for energy savings because of a force called convection. The term convection basically means that air rises as it warms. Convection occurs naturally across the globe and is best understood by the familiar term "sea breeze." For example, during summer the air above the sea is considerably cooler than that over the land. It moves naturally across the sea to the shore as the warmed air rises. This movement ends up cooling off our heavily populated sandy beaches with a rather consistent all-day sea breeze.

Although you may not actually feel the convection movement in your home, the same effect occurs there. During summer, attics capture nearly all of our home's heat, requiring attic ventilation. In winter, however, we end up losing much of our heat and have to pay for that lost energy. Installing the correct thickness of insulation is absolutely necessary. The attic ventilation system must also be designed for the climate in which the home is built. A home in Breckenridge, Colorado, has a vastly different need for insulation than does a home built in hot, humid Orlando, Florida.

Once you've improved what's termed your *building envelope* (exterior walls, windows, and roof) with better insulation and more efficient windows, your home is ready for a technologically advanced HVAC (Heating Ventilation and Air Conditioning) system. Many homes still have older systems from the 1970s and 1980s that are now in serious need of replacement.

What's exciting today is that there are many more options now than there were 20-30 years ago. Even a standard split or forced air system is nearly 40 percent more efficient than what was considered "cutting edge" back in the 1970s. The term split system describes the standard petroleum (gas or oil) fired furnace teamed up with an electric air conditioning unit that shares the home's ducting. The furnace unit is usually placed in the home's basement while the noisy air conditioning condenser box is located outside the home.

As an option, a geothermal heat pump (GHP) utilizes similar technology with a far greater level of efficiency. GHPs use the earth's natural energy to both heat and cool buildings. This option to the standard split system can cut fuel cost by nearly 50 percent and is much quieter and requires less maintenance. The primary obstacle lies within the initial cost. Although you may have to add 50 percent to the cost of installation, if you end up living in your home longer than 10 years you'll not only break even – you'll end up saving money over the second half of the GHP's life cycle. The added advantage is that the earth will also benefit from your decision to both save energy and minimize the pollution that relates to energy use.

Landscaping is another crucial aspect of green design. Although grass appears to be green, it is not when viewed from a sustainability standpoint. It requires a considerable amount of maintenance and allows precipitation to flow to streets and sewers. This effect causes local municipalities to construct substantial storm water control systems. The preferred solution is to prepare a landscaping plan that includes native plants. Trees are clearly part of that plan and can be located to help protect the home. Leafy deciduous trees can protect against extensive solar gain in the summer and evergreen trees can shield a home from winter winds. Additionally, trees help with run off and erosion.

Another landscaping solution includes rain barrels that can be attached to the roof gutters to temporarily capture rainwater for future plant irrigation. Low-lying areas on the site known as bioswales and rain gardens help retain storm water briefly and then naturally infiltrate precipitation into the aquifer below. Landscaping is a relatively inexpensive means of minimizing the use of water for irrigation supplied via utility systems. It helps save water and the energy and resources required to control and supply the water systems.

Anyone building a new home can pursue sustainable strategies, perhaps more easily. Although production of new homes requires the use of more materials than renovation, it can integrate some preferable elements such as solar orientation, site coordination, and climate-oriented strategy. The ultimate vision for sustainable design incorporates having the owner team up with the architect, the builder, and many of the other design professionals and contractors early in the design process. This promotes a holistic integration of every element of the home's configuration. At this point in the green movement, it requires more time and up-front cost, as well as a passion for and commitment to sustainability from the homeowner. The result, however, makes up for those items over time and places pioneer green homeowners in a position of environmental leadership. Ultimately, they will experience the financial benefits over a long period of time and know that they are a vital factor for saving the earth's resources.

The green homebuilding movement will vastly improve our impact on the environment, but it does not have to adversely affect the architectural expression of our communities. Those that want a very distinct and unique facade can take that direction while others can maintain their favorite style whether it be a Victorian, colonial, Craftsman, or even contemporary. It's a matter of combining personal choice with a passion to protect our environment.

David V. Hartke, AIA, MBA, LEED AP, cSBA, is a principal of Stampfl Hartke Associates, LLC, an architecture and engineering firm located in Holicong, Pennsylvania. Dave co-chairs at the Keystone Green Building Initiative (KGBI) for the Home Builders Association (HBA) of Bucks and Montgomery Counties. He is also a lead instructor for Bucks County Community College's "Substantial Building Advisor Program (SBA)."

The face and character of our country are determined
by what we do with America and its resources.
–President Thomas Jefferson

2. GREEN COTTAGES AND CABINS

Many of us revel in the idea of the cottage or the small house. Perhaps it is from perusing the fairy tales of our childhood, where all sorts of wondrous people inhabited lovely cottages. Perhaps we feel, like Thoreau, that cottage life is warm and cheery, or maybe it's all we can afford. Or perhaps we just want to downsize, to get away from suburbia or the city and sit on that porch and rock away.

Since 1965, however, the size of the average U.S. home has increased by more than 35 percent, though more than 60 percent of American households contain only one or two people. In 1965, the average home was about 1,500 square feet. Today, it is more than 2,200 square feet.

Smaller houses require less energy to heat, have a smaller environmental footprint, and are less expensive than those larger homes because they don't need as many resources (e. g., lumber, paint, windows). Smaller houses promote community and communication; everyone enjoys the one TV show together rather than each person watching their own show. In other words, small houses under 2,000 square feet such as portrayed in this chapter are not only environmentally friendly but they reduce our consumption of resources.

5-Star Austin Home & Studio

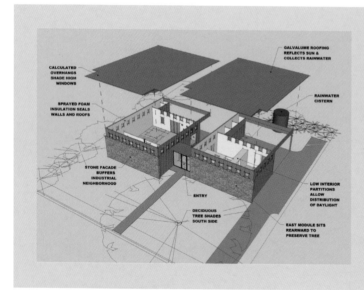

Sustainable Elements. Having a good understanding of your site and its features is essential in the development of your design. Extended site observations offer some insight into the changing sun and breeze patterns, seasonal rain and snowfall amounts, existence of wildlife, ground stability, and site drainage patterns. In developing your design, try to preserve and enhance the natural assets of your site. This exploded axon allows the viewer to see the sustainable elements in this house designed by Jackson & McElhaney Architects.

Michael McElhaney of Jackson McElhaney Architects designed an energy-efficient, low cost home and art studio on an urban Austin infill lot. He designed a home that consisted of two, similar-sized modules connected with a glass entry. Sliding pocket doors allow each of the modules to be partitioned off, while the two separate HVAC units and two separate, tankless water heaters keep the occupants comfortable. The use of a carport, instead of a garage, prevents vehicle fumes from entering the home.

One module sits rearward on the site to allow ample room for the large pecan tree, a deciduous tree providing much needed shading on the south side of the home. Large, calculated roof overhangs also protect the windows from direct sunlight. *Photo by Trey Hunter*

The two modules are centered on the site, which permits the residence to be divided into two separate houses in the future if desired. Floor plans have been drawn, and underslab plumbing installed accordingly. The entry connector could be removed, and a property line established down the center of the property. This flexibility encourages growth within the city without extensive teardown and re-building. In addition, McElhaney designed each concrete foundation to accommodate up to a three-story structure so that growth on these inner city lots can increase without causing urban sprawl. *Photo by Trey Hunter*

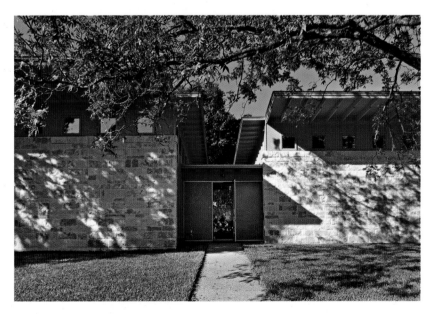

Upon entering the glass connector, the north side opens to the courtyard and its 28-foot long koi pond. Positioned in the back of the lot, the 3,000-gallon rainwater cistern collects the rainwater off the home for use in filling the koi pond and watering the landscape, resulting in substantial water savings. The windows follow the slope of the roof, framing the view of the pond. The cantilevered roof shelters the back porch, providing another place to enjoy the water garden. *Photo by Trey Hunter*

The ceilings are slatted white pine with no painted finish. This ceiling construction conceals the ducts, wiring, light fixture transformers, polyethylene plumbing piping, speakers, etc. while enhancing the acoustical quality of the rooms and keeping the ducts in the conditioned envelope of the home. The kitchen cabinet boxes, doors, and drawers comply with E-1 European emission limits for formaldehyde to help enhance the indoor air quality. Environmentally friendly pest control systems include stainless steel mesh barriers at all plumbing pipe penetrations in the slab and an inert borate and water solution sprayed on the wood framing and sheathing. *Photo by Trey Hunter*

Room-dividing walls are capped at 8 feet, allowing natural daylight to fill the rooms from small, high windows that create a continuous band around the entire house. Inserted between every other stud, these windows conserve wood because they did not require headers. *Photo by Trey Hunter*

Off-gassing. Toxins can enter your home or workplace from paint, flooring, stains, varnishes, plywood, carpeting, insulation, and other building products. These substances are released into the air through a process called off-gassing. The off-gassing can continue for years and affect your health long after construction has been completed. Today's more airtight construction methods seal in these substances rather than allowing fresh air to dilute them, which creates further problems.

The use of zero VOC paints, no coating on the wood ceiling, and no flooring materials or adhesives contribute to the enhanced indoor air quality. The spray foam insulation in the walls and ceiling provides a tight envelope, which restricts air infiltration. This type of urethane foam also keeps the air quality clean and does not contribute to off-gassing. *Photo by Trey Hunter*

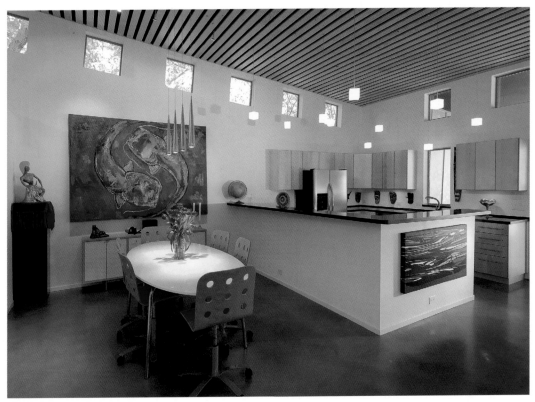

Anti-scald valves are installed at all showers to assist with the health and safety aspect of the home, while exhaust fans reduce humidity, lessening the chance of mold growth. Above-slab polyethylene tubing is installed for all water piping, which is distributed through a central manifold system. Overhead piping reduces water waste by providing direct hot water routing to each fixture and eliminates the chance of an under-slab water leak. *Photo by Trey Hunter*

The wife's art studio provides a location for her art production, which keeps her occupation in the home and doesn't require daily driving to a remote location. The studio is separately vented to keep any unwanted odors from entering the rest of the home. *Photo by Trey Hunter*

Berkeley Town House

This three-story, 1,250 square-foot town house in Berkeley, California, makes the most of a small sliver of land. It is built with wood framing, plywood sheathing, and literally dozens of hold-downs, specialized fasteners, steel strapping, and nailing designed to resist the coming earthquakes. A house in California, points out architect Bruce Kelley, is not sustainable unless it is earthquake resistant! *Courtesy of Bruce Kelley*

The passive solar elements integrated into the design – large, south-facing window, good insulation, thermal mass, curtains – all work together to reduce energy use to about one-third of the energy consumed by a conventional house in this part of the country. The south-facing window in the double-height living room provides most of the heat that the house needs. *Courtesy of Bruce Kelley*

If a very strong structure is the primary sustainable characteristic of a house in earthquake country, moisture management and water control is the next most important feature. Water and wood-framed construction do not mix well and can lead to mold, wood rot, and structural damage. Kelley & Kelley designed this house with a pressure-equalized rain screen to provide a maximum level of protection from moisture problems. This screen begins at the interior with a continuous air barrier formed by sheet rock sealed to the framing to prevent air leaks, followed by the insulation and framing, plywood sheathing, a continuous weather-resistant barrier, a 1-inch air space compartmentalized into 20-foot sections, and a final cement plaster exterior finish. Corrosion-resistant flashings protect the transitions between construction materials. Drainage paths exist to channel moisture to the exterior since all doors and windows leak eventually. With proper upkeep, the building should last indefinitely. *Courtesy of Bruce Kelley*

Thermal mass. In the architectural sense, thermal mass is any mass (e. g., concrete floors, stone and tile floors, a large boulder) that slowly absorbs and stores heat during sunny periods when the heat is not desirable in the living space of a building and then – just as slowly – releases the heat during the night or those times when the heat is desirable. A properly sized thermal mass will reduce temperature swings and help maintain comfortable temperatures throughout the day and night. Its benefits are particularly felt in climates with large daytime-to-nighttime temperature differentials.

In colder climates with a long heating season, thermal mass can also be advantageous. When the space is heated, the walls and objects in the room absorb and store the heat, which radiates to create a sense of comfort. This effect is known as "surround comfort."

The doors, floors and cabinets were all built from two recycled street trees, victims of Dutch elm disease. The walls are plaster, the handrail copper. *Courtesy of Bruce Kelley*

Designed by Brion Jeannette, this earth-sheltered home, located on the beach and next to the busy Pacific Coast Highway, is protected from heat gain and provided with nature's sound attenuation by its naturally existing rock and land exterior. The rock provides thermal mass. *Courtesy of Eric Figge. com*

A Tunisian olive jar occupies a corner of the dining patio. The ground floor is devoted to food; the second floor to living spaces; the third to a home office that overlooks the two-story living room. A roof deck provides views of San Francisco Bay and roof-level ventilation for summer cooling. *Courtesy of Bruce Kelley*

Proportion, light, and varying height make this stand-alone condominium feel generous in size. *Courtesy of Bruce Kelley*

Pioneer Cabin

With a goal of style and sustainability, Michael Heacock and the owners embarked on a 2-1/2 year journey to design and build a prefab retreat in the woods. The cabin is constructed from pre-fabricated polyurethane SIP panels in a nearby town and then assembled on site. The 800 square-foot main house and the 200 square-foot guest suite nestle comfortably within the surrounding pine forest. In addition to its modest size, the cabin nearly eliminates wood usage through innovative structural insulated wall and roof panels. *Courtesy of www. emilyhagopian. com*

An east/west breezeway with stretched fabric awnings keep both indoor and outdoor areas cool in the summer, where temperatures can rise above 90 degrees. Energy-efficient ceiling fans, along with high operable windows, assist passive cooling. *Courtesy of www. emilyhagopian. com*

Structural Insulated Panels (SIPs). SIPs are a composite building material that provides an extremely energy-efficient and airtight building envelope while minimizing the use of materials. SIPs consist of a sandwich of two layers of structural board with an insulating layer of foam in between. They share the same structural properties as an I-beam or I-column and replace several components of conventional building such as studs and joists, insulation, vapor barrier, and air barrier. As such they can be used for many different applications such as exterior wall, roof, floor, and foundation systems.

Operable windows. Windows have a tremendous environmental influence on a house, affecting the light, ventilation and temperature of the interior — and the comfort of the occupants. Today, many buildings have fixed windows so not to affect the HVAC system. The benefits of operable windows are that the homeowners have control over their environmental conditions. With the addition of fans, operable windows provide free cooling and can operate as a back-up ventilation system. *Photo © Darwin Harrison*

A tankless hot water heater supplies ample domestic hot water, and dramatically reduces energy consumption. Passive solar orientation and broad southern overhangs help keep the house cool in summer. Additional green components include energy-efficient windows, high fire resistance, and minimal site disturbance. *Courtesy of www. emilyhagopian. com*

Palmetto House

The clients, a writer and a woodworker, wanted a house that recalled the traditional "Cracker" style tin sheds of Florida with climate-responsive features. In response to this wish, Jersey Devil's design lifted it above the ground and sited it to catch the prevailing southeasterly winds in the high humidity hinterlands near the edge of the Everglades in Florida. *Courtesy of Bill Sanders*

The ground floor, which contains a woodworking studio and office, has reinforced concrete post-and-beam construction with concrete masonry infill. *Courtesy of Bill Sanders*

The upper floors, which contain the living quarters and a writer's studio on the third floor, are wood frame with an aluminum and steel skin. The house uses a radiant barrier to block up to 95 percent of the radiant heat gain: a foil barrier stapled to the outside of the wall and roof frame reflects heat. The resulting hot air is vented out through soffit, ridge, and wall vents. *Courtesy of Bill Sanders*

The upper floor has screened porches at either end, with a single room between them that contains the kitchen, living, and sleeping areas. Partitions that stop short of the ceiling divide the space. Above this space is a loft reached by a spiral staircase. Its floor is made of metal grating to help the hot air escape from the space below. *Courtesy of Bill Sanders*

Detail at eaves. *Courtesy of Bill Sanders*

The original owner was a woodworker. Although the use of wood on the exterior is minimal, the floor is made of cherry laid in wide planks, and the cabinetry is tiger maple. *Courtesy of Bill Sanders*

Texas Bungalow Revival

Ross Tedter Architect recently designed a healthy durable house that requires minimal maintenance. Featured as one of eight houses on Austin's Cool House Tour 2007 and the ninth highest rated house out of 7,500 rated by the Austin Energy Green Building Program, this traditional Texas bungalow style uses passive solar techniques that incorporate a wide traditional front porch and wide overhangs to shade windows and walls from hot Texas sun. All siding and trim is fiber cement board made from recycled wood byproducts painted with low VOC latex paint. *©2007 photo by Patrick J. Wong/Atelier Wong Photography*

The xeriscape planting beds reduce irrigation requirements with plants and soil amendments in accordance with Austin's Waterwise Landscape Rebate Program. All the eligible plants are either native or well adapted to Austin's drought-prone climate. The careful placement of the house on the narrow lot allows for morning shade provided by the red oak tree in front and pecan trees on east side. *Courtesy of Ross Tedter Architect*

VOCs. The average adult breathes approximately 13,000 liters of air each day, along with whatever harmful toxins it contains. Most conventional paints contained high levels of VOCs (volatile organic compounds) to help them dry faster. The VOCs diminish air quality and may be detrimental to your health. Choose zero-VOC paints and other products to keep indoor toxic emissions to a minimum.

The on-demand gas water heater on the east side is tucked in behind a projected wall to partially conceal the view from street. The exterior wall mounting eliminates the requirement for an expensive flue through the roof and is centrally located near plumbing fixtures to shorten time and reduce wasted water at points of use. The on-demand feature also requires much less gas usage than conventional tank water heaters. A built-in thermostat prevents winter freezing of waterlines. *Courtesy of Ross Tedter Architect*

The kitchen has maintenance-free and antibacterial manmade quartz countertops. The under-cabinet and above-cabinet lighting is energy-efficient fluorescent strip lighting with electronic ballasts. The kitchen floor is interlocking cork planking with a high-density fiberboard core laid over a vinyl sheet vapor barrier sprinkled with earth-friendly borate for pest control. Resilient and moisture-resistant, durable cork is taken from the bark of cork oak trees without killing the trees. *Courtesy of Ross Tedter Architect*

The dining and living room area has multi-ply, glue-down, pre-finished oak veneer plank flooring, wood frame windows with insulated low-emissive glazing, and extruded fiberglass exterior that provide excellent resistance to solar heat gain and winter cold. Zero VOC latex paint is used for all interior wall and trim. The cellular window shades provide privacy and additional energy-saving sun control. *©2007 photo by Patrick J. Wong/Atelier Wong Photography*

The HVAC closet in the centrally located downstairs hall contains stacked air handler unit (combined electric spilt-system air conditioner and gas furnace) set on built-up deck with return air grille below. The pleated media filter tray is shown partially open with a dampered foil-faced fresh air duct to the right that permits controlled mixing of outside air with return air before it enters the unit. The location of the return air at the first floor works well for the long cooling season in Austin's hot and humid climate. The split system air conditioning system has an outside condenser unit that sits on a concrete pad on the east side of the house and suction and refrigerant lines that circulate to the air handler unit inside. *Courtesy of Ross Tedter Architect*

The sealed and fully insulated attic has a minimum of 5-inch thick (minimum R-19) soy-based urethane foam blown insulation applied to underside of roof decking; the insulated attic space keeps summer temperatures below 85 degrees Fahrenheit. Consequently, the HVAC cooling load is greatly reduced because the ductwork passes through mild attic space. The entire house is insulated with the same insulation, providing a tightly sealed and well-insulated envelope. *Courtesy of Ross Tedter Architect*

Strobel Casita

Designed by Boor Bridges Architecture as a defensible 1,200 square-foot compound for a single, retired woman, this house sits in the rough-hewn chaparral of the upper Mexican plateau. Three pavilions organize the house into areas for working, living, and sleeping. A series of walls and courtyards join the pavilions together to create substantial outdoor living space and circulation. The rock plinth on the south side of the house forms an outdoor porch, overlooking the verdant agricultural valley below. *Courtesy of Robert DeGast & Boor Bridges Architecture.*

The siting of the house takes advantage of the sun to avoid over-heating. Composed of a double layer of brick, the south wall insulates the house during the day and radiates heat during cool desert nights. Prevailing winds help maintain a comfortable interior temperature during the day. Xeriscaping a small area outside the house eliminates the need for irrigation. *Courtesy of Robert DeGast & Boor Bridges Architecture*

This house captures the essence of what it means to build in the upper plateau of Mexico: peaceful indoor/outdoor living. Interior gardens placed near the kitchen and bathroom use direct graywater for irrigation. *Courtesy of Robert DeGast & Boor Bridges Architecture*

Greywater. To reduce the impact on wells or water treatments plants, "Greywater" or wastewater from dishwashing or washing machines can be used to flush toilets, water lawns, and wash cars. A separate plumbing system is used to collect greywater.

High barrel-vaulted ceilings made of native brick help cool the house during the day and keep it warm at night. *Courtesy of Robert DeGast & Boor Bridges Architecture*

Located on a four-acre site about five miles from town, the house is "off-the-grid" and incorporates many sustainable design elements. The walls and roofs are constructed of tabique, a native low-fire clay brick that absorbs heat during the day and re-radiates it at night. Water harvested from the roof passes through a three-part charcoal filter and is stored in a cistern below the ground. Pumping the water back to the roof into a holding tank creates pressure for distribution throughout the house. *Courtesy of Robert DeGast & Boor Bridges Architecture*

Generated from the shower and sink, recycled graywater waters an adjacent garden. The technology is minimal: the water simply drains into the garden. *Courtesy of Robert DeGast & Boor Bridges Architecture*

Brick ceilings and walls insulate and store heat for cool nights. *Courtesy of Robert DeGast & Boor Bridges Architecture*

Five solar photovoltaic arrays provide the majority of electricity to this completely off-the-grid home. Propane provides back up heat to fireplaces on cold winter nights. A large cistern collects water run-off from the roof, filtering and pumping it back to the roof where it is gravity fed to the house. *Courtesy of Robert DeGast & Boor Bridges Architecture*

Awnings provide shaded areas around the house and allow movement between the pavilions during inclement weather. The breezeways connecting the compound's three pavilions eliminate the need for a supplemental cooling system. *Courtesy of Robert DeGast & Boor Bridges Architecture*

Rhode Island Beach House

Designed by Gary Graham, FAIA, this small residence in New England's coastal zone represents an innovative approach to the contemporary beach house. Designed to be a comfortable, livable, year-round home for a professional couple, it also incorporates a concept of sensible sustainability. *Courtesy of www. brucetmartin. com*

Exterior materials were selected for performance and environmental purposes. The metal roof has a long life and performs well in hurricanes; its light, reflective color reduces the need for artificial cooling. The sustainably harvested white cedar shingles are consistent with New England coastal architecture and did not require shipping from the west coast. The cedar strips are used as both a rain screen protection layer on the kitchen extension and a visual screen on the free-standing stair tower. *Courtesy of www. brucetmartin. com*

Current regulations require all structures in the coastal zone to be designed to withstand the lateral forces of wind and waves. The 2-½ story structure was built on piers with breakaway glass block infill walls at the lower level. Because non-reinforced masonry is allowed as a breakaway wall methodology, the use of glass blocks not only meets the regulatory requirement, but also provides transparency on the lower level to enhance the concept of a house that floats above the ground. *Courtesy of www. brucetmartin. com*

Graham addressed lateral forces in his beach house design with two concrete shear walls on the lowest level, pressure-treated wood piers with a stainless steel bracket and tension cable bracing system, and a series of plywood "sandwich" shear walls on the upper levels. *Courtesy of Gary Graham*

This home has just 1,700 square feet of living space plus an additional 1,000 square feet of "non-occupiable" space on the ground floor for a heated storage/workshop space and an unheated garage. This passive solar home will become an active solar house, when a "peel and stick" photovoltaic solar array is added to the south-facing metal roof once the State of Rhode Island enacts pending solar incentives. *Courtesy of www. brucetmartin. com*

The home includes a sensitive selection of sustainable materials such as bamboo, slate, and travertine tile floors. Located next to the south-facing window wall, the travertine acts as a passive radiant heat source by absorbing the rays of the sun. The tile also acts as a hearth for the sealed, gas-fired furnace/fireplace, which is a secondary heat source for the entire house. Note the almost invisible Runtal baseboard radiator that is part of the home's perimeter hydronic hot water system, powered by a 95% efficient, European compact condensing boiler. *Courtesy of www. brucetmartin. com*

The site came with a mandate to take advantage of the beautiful views. Every room in this new home is oriented to take advantage of the many moods of the sea and sky. Moreover, the large windows on the southern side of the house are carefully positioned to utilize the sun to help warm the house in the winter months. *Courtesy of www. brucetmartin. com*

Architect Gary Graham maximized the effective "R" value of the exterior skin of the house by utilizing a 2 x 6 advanced wood framing system that reduces the amount of wood, and increases the area available for the icyenene foam insulation. *Courtesy of Gary Graham*

Thermal envelope technology. There are many techniques available. Homeowner Sean Neilson says, "The pink foam sheathing on the entire house in our home in Gustavus, Alaska (note the bear!), helps us keep in the heat, which is solely generated from a woodstove." Foam sheathing, an advancement in thermal envelope technology, can help consumers to absorb today's higher energy costs. *Courtesy of Sean Neilson*

A Passively Cool Surf Shack

William Hoffman designed this house to "touch the earth lightly." Individual, somewhat elevated, freely elongated house types are preferred in the south Florida subtropical climate, where high temperature conditions prevail. The natural remedy for such a situation lies in increased air movement; therefore, the utilization of wind effects is the primary consideration in site selection. For sun orientation, where overheated conditions prevail practically all year long, exposures with minimum solar heat intake are advantageous. A position very near to the east-west axis is desirable. *Courtesy of Bill Sanders*

In a subtropical climate region, walls are used primarily for screening from insects and for their wind penetration qualities rather than thermal barriers. The covered entry vestibule opens to the kitchen and living room through adjoining French doors. The covered, screen-enclosed transitional spaces at the front and rear of the house provide sun, rain and critter protection, while the open exterior wall allows for the maximum airflow. *Courtesy of Bill Sanders*

The kitchen opens wide to the dining and living rooms. Any form of heat storage is avoided by removing interior walls when possible, inducing cross ventilation. Increasing the airflow modulates temperature and humidity, bringing the environment into the "comfort zone." *Courtesy of Bill Sanders*

Interior spaces are shaded and well ventilated to maintain comfortable interior temperatures. To induce cross ventilation through all the interior spaces, the distance in the north to south direction is kept to a minimum for the entire length of the house. *Courtesy of Bill Sanders*

To maintain comfort, interior spaces must be shaded and well ventilated. The master bedroom opens to a south-facing covered screened enclosure and a screened shade house to the north, providing cross ventilation. This fern/orchid filled shaded space can be seen from the master bedroom. It provides passive cooling and serves as an insect protection transition space to the exterior. A large stand of bamboo shades the east windows from the heat of the low rising eastern sun. The garage was broken out as a separate form to promote airflow and create a privacy space for the master bedroom from the street. *Courtesy of Bill Sanders*

To provide a comfortable interior environment in a hot humid environment, the temperature and humidity must be reduced. Ideally, the long south face of a structure faces the prevailing breeze with the short sides facing east and west. The breeze passing over a water body (the Atlantic Ocean in this case) and then passing under high branching trees reduces the air temperature before passing through the interior spaces of the house. Screened transitional spaces include the south-facing covered deck, which runs the length of the full house. All interior spaces open into this space through adjoining French doors. *Courtesy of Bill Sanders*

To promote airflow, especially on those "dead air" days, an elongated windowed cupola at the roof ridge creates a "stack" effect to thermally induce airflow, with additional help from reversible blade ceiling fans. Louvered vents are located above interior doors to promote air movement further through the house. *Courtesy of Bill Sanders*

The roof takes on the strongest thermal impacts. It must be water tight, insulated, and reflective. This roof is vaulted on the interior, with an insulted double roof above, and a reflective "5V crimp" galvalume roof covering to the exterior. To further promote free air movement and to visually lighten the form, the house and screened enclosures are elevated off the ground. *Courtesy of Bill Sanders*

On the north and east sides, the 13-foot-high house is built into the ground. The north and east walls are made of concrete, which absorbs the ground's constant 52-degree Fahrenheit temperature and cools the house in the summer by slowly emitting chilled air into the house. The canopy prevents morning and evening sun from heating up the structure, and lofty trees block the high daytime sun. *Courtesy of Jeff Heatley*

Architect Edvin Stromsten set out to build a 1,600-square-foot, zero energy home dwelling in East Hampton, N. Y. To obtain super energy efficiency, Stromsten focused on orientation, earth sheltering, thermal mass, super insulation, geothermal heating and cooling, and photovoltaic electrical generation. The house requires no fossil fuel. *Courtesy of Jeff Heatley*

During the winter when the sun is lower in the sky, the home is flooded with solar energy. In the summer, when the sun is at a higher point, a small overhang shades the home from direct sunlight. *Courtesy of Jeff Heatley*

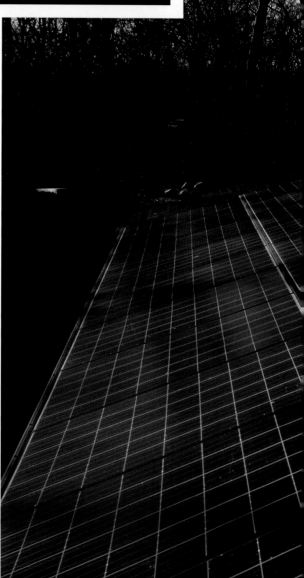

The home was also constructed with ample thermal mass. The concrete floors and walls are especially effective in the winter, absorbing heat from the low winter sun during the day and slowly releasing that heat throughout the night. *Courtesy of Jeff Heatley*

Stromsten oriented the home so most of the glass faces south. *Courtesy of Jeff Heatley*

47

During the day, no electric lights are needed. *Courtesy of Jeff Heatley*

The light-filled spacious home has cathedral ceilings throughout. *Courtesy of Jeff Heatley*

The predominant materials are concrete walls, polished concrete floors with stucco, and sheetrock as required. *Courtesy of Jeff Heatley*

The low-E tempered insulating windows connect the house closely to the outdoors. *Courtesy of Jeff Heatley*

To minimize energy consumption even more, Stromsten installed a geothermal system using an open-loop system to provide heating and cooling and hot water to the home. A $2,200 rebate from the Long Island Power Authority (LIPA) covered a good deal of the installation cost. Another $15,000 rebate from LIPA covered about half the cost of installing a 3.75-kilowatt panel of photovoltaic cells, which generates enough power to run the geothermal system, a refrigerator, and minimum amount of domestic electricity. *Courtesy of Jeff Heatley*

Using the latest green, sustainable technology, the so-called "zero emissions house" is environmentally friendly and produces 90 percent of the energy it needs to warm and cool the house, power appliances, and keep the lights on after dark. *Courtesy of Jeff Heatley*

3. THOSE IN BETWEEN

Wisconsin High Performance Residence

Our houses define the way we live – and the way we want to live. After all, many houses have dining rooms, but how often are they really used? Still, owning a dining room may be part of our dream for ourselves. We expect our house to perform many roles and provide a variety of finely designed spaces. Although the upfront costs may be high, green houses are less costly to maintain. They benefit from lower utility costs and greater energy independence and provide better indoor air quality than houses built to conventional standards and codes. The question is whether we want to live green?

This view shows the living room window, lower level walkout, and upper level central belvedere loft for passive cooling. The 100-year site-built standing-seam metal roof is not only made of recycled steel but is fully recyclable. Built by Gimme Shelter Construction, the home does not have any plywood, OSB, or engineered panel products. *Courtesy of Tom Brown*

Architect Thomas Brown designed this award-winning residence in central Wisconsin, a cold climate region. The National Association of Homebuilders Research Center (NAHBRC) awarded his design the First-place Gold Energy Value 2000 Award. It was deemed the best Innovative/Advanced residence in a cold-climate region in the U. S. It also received a 5-Star PLUS rating under the EPA Energy Star Homes program. *Courtesy of Mike & Melba Sullivan*

Building Envelopes. Brown's design for a superinsulated home employs a variation on conventional wood-frame construction to create a certifiably airtight building envelope. A layer of interior horizontal "strapping" reduces the solid-wood conductive content of the wall, creating a thermal break between the inside and outside wall surfaces and allowing for higher levels of insulation. A layer of exterior "furring" over the sheathing creates a "rain screen" for weather resistance and long-term durability of the wood siding. *Courtesy of Tom Brown*

The all-electric house is 1,936 sq. ft. in area on the main level, with a partially finished lower level and a heated garage workshop, for a total heated area of 3,820 sq. ft. The house orientation is optimized for passive solar heating, while roof overhangs and window placement allow summer cooling.

This view from airlock entry towards the belvedere loft stairway shows the salvaged structural posts and glue-laminated beams, which were used to avoid consuming old growth timber. Locally produced shiplap wood planking is used for all floor, wall, and roof sheathing to allow for future "de-construction" of the home. The use of this planking also eliminates all plywood or composite panel products, which contain urea formaldehyde glues. *Courtesy of Tom Brown*

Hydronic Radiant Floors. Radiant floors are a popular heating alternative to forced air systems. They offer comfort, ease of use, low maintenance, and efficiency. They are particularly good in rugless houses because the floor will keep your feet warm. They do not work as well if you use a carpet because its insulating nature hampers the floor's efficiency.

This image shows the radiant tubing laid out on a wood deck. The tubes will be embedded in a 3-inch concrete slab, which also provides useful passive solar thermal mass for keeping temperatures even and storing heat. The thermal mass also helps keep the house cool in summer.

The hydronic radiant heating is coupled with a closed-loop ground-source geothermal heat pump. Heat recovery ventilation ensures good indoor air quality. A high efficiency central masonry heater provides back up heating. This all-electric home has had excellent overall thermal performance for this climate. *Courtesy of Tom Brown*

California Hill House

Notice the trees to the left? In keeping with the principles of green architecture, the owners milled and dried on location the entire exterior siding and trim for the house. *photos by j. nichole. com*

Generous window openings, along with surfaces that extend outdoors, allow the occupants to feel that they are at home amid the surrounding ninety-year-old cedars. In the background, the moveable storage wall acts to create a backdrop for the dining table and separates the main living spaces from a semi-private studio/library – while providing substantial internal storage on a rolling chassis! *Courtesy of Juan Hernandez*

Coates used ground-face concrete masonry units to shape the entry enclosure. They also add thermal mass, which helps to keep temperatures stabilized throughout the day. *photos by j. nichole. com*

Coates Design Architects oriented this site-sensitive house to make use of passive solar design. Its thick masonry walls function as thermal collectors to help stabilize temperatures. *photos by j. nichole. com*

The low maintenance concrete floor allows the structural slab to double as the finish floor. Hydronic radiant tubes in the slab heat the house. This thermal mass keeps temperatures in the house stabilized throughout the day. *Courtesy of Juan Hernandez*

The exposed structure of the room results in less drywall and maintenance- intensive finishes. Water- and energy efficient appliances, a light dimming system, and hydronic heating are some of the sustainable features of the house. The owners poured their own concrete countertops, another sustainable element.

The up-lights give a pleasing quality of light as it is reflected from the wood ceiling. The light is warmed and bounced evenly in the living space, making it easier on the eyes and creating a sense of coziness. *Courtesy of Juan Hernandez*

Regionally Sourced Materials. Sustainable design minimizes importation of goods and energy and works in harmony with the natural features and resources surrounding the proposed site. It uses renewable indigenous building materials where feasible.

The wall opening provides glimpses to the trees outside at the top of the stairs and also improves communication between people within the house. No longer does one person have to shout down the stairs to another! *Courtesy of Juan Hernandez*

Point White Residence

Sited on a ridge top, 10 miles from the Pacific Ocean, the Hill House looks like a giant smile carved into the hillside. The house, designed by Jersey Devil Architects, a nomadic group of design-and-build architect contractors, is cut into the crest of the ridge to present a low profile to coastal storms. Winds in this area can be more than 100 miles per hour. The house sits in a south-facing bowl, allowing the wind to move over it while still permitting generous sunlight. *Courtesy of Steve Badanes, Jersey Devil Architects*

The southwest-facing side of the house is a glass wall that provides spectacular views of the mountains and forms part of a passive solar heating and cooling system. An 8-inch thick Trombe wall beneath the windows also collects and conducts heat into the house. A windmill pumps water to a storage tank, and the water is gravity fed to the house. Domestic hot water is solar heated. *Courtesy of Steve Badanes, Jersey Devil Architects*

By following the contours of the ridge and using earth berms, stone from the site, and a living roof, the house blends into the natural terrain. This strategy provides fire, wind, and earthquake resistance as well as reducing heating and cooling loads. Thermal mass construction and earth integration help to mitigate temperature swings. *Courtesy of Steve Badanes, Jersey Devil Architects*

Even in the summer, the Hill House is always cool – thanks to its buried form. The sod roof is apparent in this view. *Courtesy of Steve Badanes, Jersey Devil Architects*

Other materials used in the house such as the concrete walls, quarry-tiled concrete floor, stone, and stucco partitions provide thermal mass so to stabilize temperatures. *Courtesy of Steve Badanes, Jersey Devil Architects*

An Environmentally Responsible House

Holzman Moss Architecture designed this house to meet the U.S. Green Building Council LEED pilot residential requirements. It is divided into two rectangles that have been shifted out of alignment to improve natural ventilation, light, and views and to reduce the scale of the house. Displacing the main volumes of the house allows for more daylight and ventilation to enter the interior. *Photo © Darwin Harrison*

The sloped roof mimics the contours of the land. Photovoltaic panels on the roof produce energy for the house. At dusk, the building glows. *Photo © Darwin Harrison*

LEED. The Leadership in Energy and Environmental Design rating system (LEED) from the U. S. Green Building Council (USGBC) is a system that rates buildings for their environmental sustainability. By its definition, a green home uses less energy, water, and resources and creates less waste such as greenhouse gas emissions. A home can qualify if it meets minimum criteria under a points system. Credit is given for features such as energy-efficient insulation and water heaters, water-efficient toilets and fixtures, and use of resources such as readily procurable and sustainable materials and long-lasting siding. Houses are rated on seven criteria: location and linkages, sustainable site, water efficiency, indoor environmental quality, materials and resources, energy and atmosphere, and homeowner awareness.

According to the *Wall Street Journal* (September 21, 2007, p. B 6), developers are eager to secure the benefits that result from this green seal of approval. The program requires third-party inspection and commissioning before certification.

Some architects and environmentalists point out that the nonprofit council should be "asking far more of buildings granted LEED certification. Buildings that have won LEED certification achieved an average 25 -to 30-percent reduction in energy use — a significant savings but less than the 50 percent that a group of prominent architectural firms recently declared necessary and achievable."

The critics point out that current criteria also do not recognize regional differences. For example, conserving water contributes equally to a building's rating in rainy Seattle as it does in dry Tucson. They also point out that the system allows developers to be rated higher for installing new technologies such as solar panels, which, while important, don't achieve as much in energy savings as good insulation and an airtight facade.

Others point out that it took only seven years, from the launch of the LEED program in 2000, for green buildings to have an impact on the residential market. Hopefully, it will have a greater impact in the future.

Meanwhile, the National Association of Homebuilders is developing its own standards, which, according to *The Wall Street Journal* (Thursday, November 8, 2007. D.1) are flexible, depending on the region and include easier to achieve certification. The federal government's Energy Star program also certifies homes that meet a standard on energy use. The 2007 yardstick is at least 15 percent more efficient than homes built to the 2004 residential code.

The child's slide leading directly from the playroom to the outdoors underscores the fluidity between internal and external spaces. Holzman Moss Architecture developed a new approach known as Utilicores to prefabricated architecture by placing the bathrooms, kitchen, laundry, and mechanical units into a single module, which resulted in an increased construction speed and reduced project costs. *Photo © Darwin Harrison*

Flooring materials used throughout the house are produced from rapidly renewable or recycled products such as bamboo, cork, and re-claimed wood. *Photo © Darwin Harrison*

The interior of the house was conceived as two large loft-like rooms. Both have high ceilings reflecting the shape of the house, exposing the roof structure and wood ceiling decking. One is dedicated to the children, including bedrooms, playroom, library, storage, and bath. Exposed energy-saving compact fluorescent light bulbs are utilized as cost-effective light fixtures throughout the house. *Photo © Darwin Harrison*

The other includes a gathering area, kitchen, dining, and master bedroom suite. The homeowner's extensive scavenging of reclaimed building materials benefited the project's aesthetic, cost, and sustainability. Marble toilet partitions found in a salvage yard are used as kitchen countertops; custom-designed wood doors not used for another project serve as interior doorways. *Photo © Darwin Harrison*

Chromacolor House

This ecologically sustainable home, designed by Translation of Space, is a progressive dwelling for modern living. Its energy-efficient envelope is wrapped in cement board siding, sand finish stucco, spruce, and aluminum. This home was designed to meet a USGBC rating, LEED silver certification. *Courtesy of Kevin Rolly*

Its modest size (2,400 square feet of living space spread over two stories), height, and overall density are sensitive to the fabric of the surrounding neighborhood. *Courtesy of Kevin Rolly*

Its U-shaped floor plan wraps around the north-facing courtyard, allowing indirect sunlight and ventilation to penetrate every interior space. The reverse floor plan puts private spaces on the lower level and common spaces upstairs to take advantage of direct sunlight, ocean breezes, and views. The ceilings are 9 feet throughout, while 12-feet high stair and kitchen volumes act as passive cooling ventilation towers. The warmest air is drawn up into the towers and out through operable clerestory windows. Opposing operable windows and doors are designed to thread cross ventilation through each of the building's spaces. *Courtesy of Kevin Rolly*

Clerestory. The upper part of a building whose walls contain windows specifically intended to provide lighting to the interior.

The stained plywood and plate steel staircase meet smooth, polished fly ash concrete and a soy-based glossy sealer. *Courtesy of Kevin Rolly*

Porous groundcover and drought-tolerant plant material live in harmony with a steel and concrete recirculating water feature. *Courtesy of Kevin Rolly*

The sustainable characteristics range from the soy-based floor sealer and low VOC paint, to the composite floor system, fly ash concrete, and dual-flush toilets. Many of its passive elements are the derivative of a small, modest, site-sensitive building. Its active elements include a radiant floor heating system, tankless water heater, Energy Star appliances, and a 1-kilowatt array of photovoltaic panels that generate approximately 30 percent of this building's energy needs. *Courtesy of Kevin Rolly*

Colorado East Bridge Sunrise

Doug Graybeal, Architect, designed this energy-efficient, environmentally friendly residence outside of Carbondale, Colorado, a dry mountain environment. Integrating the 2,463 square-foot house into the natural features of the site, he placed it over an abandoned road cut. *Courtesy of Pat Sudmeier*

Heated by passive solar energy, the house is designed to maximize the outstanding southern views of the Elk Mountain range. Concrete floors provide thermal mass and incorporate radiant heat tubes for the backup conventional heating system (as required by mortgage companies). A 2-foot thick cast earth wall provides additional thermal mass. This wall also divides the living spaces from secondary uses. *Courtesy of Pat Sudmeier*

Certified plantation-growth cherry cabinets and granite quarried in North Dakota highlight the kitchen, while energy-efficient compact fluorescent light provides an over-all glow to the main interior space. *Courtesy of Pat Sudmeier*

A continuous central cast earth wall provides thermal mass to all the main level spaces, buffering summer and winter temperature swings. Recessed wall nooks prove space for art and lighting. *Courtesy of Pat Sudmeier*

A simple piece of local Colorado sandstone with a metal backsplash and back lite local glass bowl sink create a unique powder room feature. *Courtesy of Pat Sudmeier*

A corrugated metal roof provides summer sun control as it reflects sunlight through upper windows to provide natural daylight deep into the interior. *Courtesy of Pat Sudmeier*

Found or recycled objects. The greenhouse sink is made from an old galvanized bucket. Green architecture often incorporates manufactured items or natural objects in an artistic manner. *Courtesy of Pat Sudmeier*

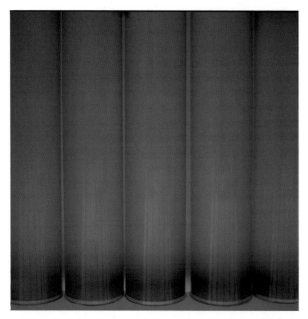

The attached greenhouse beyond provides vegetables year around without backup heat. The water tubes and circulation of hot air from the top of the greenhouse through rock beds under the planting soils will keep the greenhouse comfortable for plant growth year around. *Courtesy of Pat Sudmeier*

Green House in an Orange Grove

Thompson-Naylor Architects designed this 2,000 square-foot residence located in the center of an existing orange grove. They oriented the house to maximize solar efficiency and constructed it with SIPs instead of conventional framing. This view of the north side shows the integral color plaster and metal roof. The house includes water-efficient kitchen and bathroom fixtures and a tankless water heater. *Photography by Ryan Siphers, Deepn Jain, Sebastian Romero, and Stephanie Tracey*

This view is of the living room looking west. The exposed concrete floor contains an in-floor (slab) hydronic radiant heating system, which prevents dust, pollen, etc., from infiltrating the interior. The high performance windows allow cross ventilation and abundant daylight and provide great mountain views. *Courtesy of www. emilyhagopian. com*

The kitchen has a bamboo breakfast bar, Slatescape countertops, and wheatboard cabinets. *Courtesy of www. emilyhagopian. com*

Note the sunflower seed desk countertop. The shelving is formaldehyde-free, and non-toxic sealants, adhesives and oils were used. *Courtesy of www.emilyhagopian.com.*

Durable Building Materials and Finishes. Put down those hardwoods; plants and crops are being harvested into durable building materials and finishes. Less prone to warping than conventional lumber, green-engineered lumber products are composite materials made with wood chips and other wood waste.

Rapidly renewable bamboo, cork, wheatboard, sunflower seeds, and sorghum stalks are among the many new materials being used.

DESERT OUTPOST

After reclaiming an old dump, Steve Badanes and Jim Adamson of Jersey Devil built an exotic retirement home in Palm Springs, California. The house has two wings, one of which includes separate guest quarters and a garage to keep the vehicles out of the sun, with a west-facing courtyard under a curving canopy. *Courtesy of Steve Badanes*

The house is all about outdoor living, and its primary room is the space that surrounds the lap pool in the courtyard under the canopy. Partly sheltered and party open, the house has places that can be enjoyed in every season – even in the Palm Springs summer! *Courtesy of Steve Badanes*

A lipstick red trellis ends over the pool in a knife-edge waterfall that provides evaporative cooling for the courtyard. *Courtesy of Steve Badanes*

The two wings are opposing sheds, framed with prefabricated trusses. A layer of insulation atop the ceilings and radiant barriers between the tops of the trusses and the underside of the roof deck protect the living spaces from the Palm Springs heat. Concealed in the overhangs on the sides of the house, motorized exterior shades protect the house when the temperatures really soar. *Courtesy of Steve Badanes*

SAN FRANCISCO BAY RESIDENCE

Michael Heacock designed this award-winning 2,000 square-foot residence on San Francisco Bay. The house features many green materials and sustainable design strategies, such as a high efficiency gas furnace and hydronic radiant floor heat in the studio, SIP panels, double pane low-E wood-clad windows, and a modest size. *Courtesy of www. emilyhagopian. com*

The clients recycled and reused as many materials as possible. For example, the house used salvaged material from the previous house and has FSC certified Brazilian cherry flooring and reclaimed lumber from Utah. *Courtesy of www. emilyhagopian. com*

The kitchen boosts a reclaimed black acacia island countertop, Energy Star appliances, durable stainless steel finishes, and abundant daylighting. *Courtesy of www. emilyhagopian. com*

Forest Stewardship Council Certified (FSC). Logging practices can have negative impacts such as destroying habitats, polluting water, and displacing indigenous peoples. Many forest products companies and consumers believe that logging can be managed responsibly and that forests can be protected. An international organization, the Forest Stewardship Council was created to increase the practice of sustainable forestry worldwide. FSC certification means that the products come from a certified well-managed forest.

Note the translucent screen between the bedroom and bath. *Courtesy of www. emilyhagopian. com*

Minimal site disturbance allowed the beautiful gardens to flourish through the construction process. The reclaimed redwood siding and entry stair, abundant daylighting, and innovative glass awning detail compliment the interior hardware and island design. *Courtesy of www. emilyhagopian. com*

From Sows to Solar

A winner in the National Passive Solar Residential Design and Demonstration Competition sponsored by the Department of Housing and Urban Development and a similar design contest in Iowa, this residence, designed by David Block, was the first, scientifically designed, passive solar house in Iowa. It was intended to portray direct-gain passive solar parts and principles. The entire south wall is glass (the collector), the floor is hollow core concrete slabs (the mass), and the entire upper level is open (convective loops).

This autumn twilight view shows how the 2,200 square-foot two-story house was sunken into a previously flat site, with a dished area in front of the glass to further solar radiation gain. Bridges to the main level (the upper level), which is the public area of the house, permit entrances and exits. The heating cost for the entire first winter was under $45.00. *Photo by Dr. Laurent Hodges*

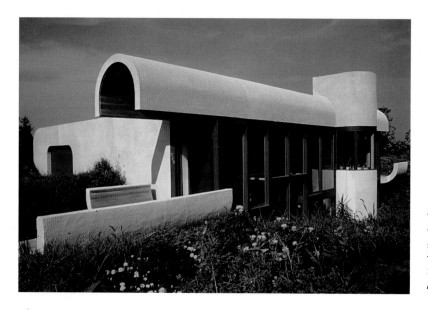

The exterior view shows the integration of the summer flowers and earth around the stucco house. Block incorporated rounded forms to remind the client of beloved Southwestern American architectural forms. *Photo by David Block AIA*

The north wall is completely covered with earth; one and a half stories of the two-story west elevation are bermed; and the house appears to be a one-story home. The garage on the north also buffers against cold northwest Iowa winter winds. *Photo by David Block AIA*

The entrance to the lower level is via the circular stairway on the left, which connects to a hallway that runs much of the length of the house. Since the hallway is immediately next to the glass, the space is exciting, well lit, and also functions as a plant area. The airflow holes in the main floor are clearly evident on the upper right. *Photo by David Block AIA*

Upon entering the home from the southwest, a visitor is greeted by the no knot fir wood barrel vault ceiling and interesting sun shadows on the floor. There is visual as well as air passage between the two floors, which facilitates the passive solar airflow into the hollow core floor structure. *Photo by David Block AIA*

SIZE MATTERS

Lindy Small Architecture designed this 2,000 square-foot house in Palo Alto, California. Large concrete pavers, flanked by drought-resistant landscaping of manzanita trees, lead to the entry of the house. The interior light scoops are visible from the approach, and a landscape screen of certified ipe wood at the front door signals that the house and garden are essential to each other. *Courtesy of www. emilyhagopian. com*

Among the ideas tested in this design was the desire to produce radiance within the space: space being considered both as interior and exterior space. Or in other words, is this a House in a Garden or a Garden with a House? The house and the landscape are essential to each other, and the interior and exterior spaces flow together. *Courtesy of www. emilyhagopian. com*

The central public space contains the living room, dining room, and kitchen. The corner "Moroccan Room" is Small's response to the clients' desire for an intimate space within the larger public space. The flat ceiling plane is punctuated by two-barrel vaults, wrapped in certified maple plywood, which admit interior light and help define the living, dining, and kitchen spaces. *Courtesy of www. emilyhagopian. com*

The house opens onto a drought-resistant garden designed by Landscape Architect Bernard Trainor. The landscape plays off the interior materials: the plantings are arranged to create a strong visual connection to the clarity of interior materials. Custom-designed certified ipe wood awnings installed over tinted doors and windows modify the light infiltration to the interior. *Courtesy of www. emilyhagopian. com*

Concrete countertops and exterior concrete pavers echo the home's radiant concrete floor, and the simplicity of the interior materials is reflected in bold plantings. Small's attention to sun angles at different times of the year, together with high-value cellulose insulation, contributes to the maintenance of a constant interior temperature. *Courtesy of www. emilyhagopian. com*

Windy Ridge House

Linda Kiisk, AIA LEED AP, designed this 2,400 square-foot home to nestle below a ridge, which has panoramic views of the Laramie River Valley. Laramie is 7,200 feet above sea level, and it snows even in August. The area has little rainfall, which leads to extremely dry conditions. Its open spaces promote strong winds, often gusting to 50 to 75 miles per hour across the plains. The air is fresh, and, according to Kiisk, the stars sparkle like no other place on the planet.

She designed the three-bedroom home to capture the spectacular south- and east-facing views and daylight, while blocking the extreme winds coming from the west. The colors of the house are selected to echo the color of the local soils. *Courtesy of Jess W. Smith, 2007*

Straw Bale Construction. Straw bale buildings can reduce wood use, increase energy and water savings, support local economies, and are a cheap solution to housing needs. The thick walls resulting from straw bale give designers, such as Architect Linda Kiisk, opportunities to play with texture and form, light, and shadow. *Courtesy of Jess W. Smith, 2007*

The walls are hybrid straw bale – three string bales (baled locally) weighing approximately 60 pounds each and measuring 3 feet by 18 inch by 18 inch. They are stacked six bales high and then impaled by two metal rods and bolted to wood boards. These three-foot-wide straw bale stacks are then set between 2 x 6 wood stud framing and easily attached to the roof and floor structure. The bales are plastered on the inside and stuccoed on the outside. The building style and construction are extremely simple; the builder can set up the bales for the house and its roof even in the roaring winds. *Courtesy of Jess W. Smith, 2007*

This truth window shows the straw bale construction. *Courtesy of Jess W. Smith, 2007*

The floor in the hall shown here is hickory. *Courtesy of Jess W. Smith, 2007*

The furniture maker who operates his business next door supplied locally harvested wood for the peeled log posts on the porch. The downspouts are chains. *Courtesy of Jess W. Smith, 2007*

Gas fireplaces supply the heat for the home. *Courtesy of Jess W. Smith, 2007*

A Rinnai continuous-flow, tankless water heater supplies all of the hot water for the home. *Courtesy of Jess W. Smith, 2007*

The MA House

Hays+Ewing Design Studio designed this 2,500 square-foot ecologically intelligent house for their use. Located in Charlottesville, Virginia, the house draws inspiration from houses in Japan and Europe, where they both lived and studied. As former partners at William McDonough and Partners, the house also embodies their depth of experience in green building technologies. There are numerous strategies at work in the house: some influence the well being of the family members; others positively affect their health; and still others contribute to the health of the environment. © *Prakash Patel*

Two Japanese concepts of space provided the conceptual framework for the design of the house. The first, known as *ma*, refers to the spatial interval between two objects or two edges. The second, *hashi*, refers to bridging the two edges. These edges can be either physical – like chopsticks bridging between the plate and the mouth – or symbolic, spanning between the secular world and the heavenly world. Located in an old mill village, this house is itself a place between; it feels both urbane (little more than a mile from downtown) and pastoral (the flood plains deter high-density development); it acts as the bridge spanning between the urbane and pastoral, public and private. The house is split in two parts with a bridge spanning over the entry court. The bridge is a place of transition and connectivity, both joining and separating the public and private spaces within the house while expanding the boundaries of the interior to the outdoors. From the entry, the bridge and flanking structure frame a view of the landscape. © *Prakash Patel*

Stormwater, when directed into storm drains, typically can overload the municipal stormwater system and pollute waterways. Hays + Ewing sought to naturally treat stormwater on their site: rainwater is collected from the roofs of the house and directed to a channel planted with native blue flag irises. Their roots absorb toxins from stormwater. A constructed wetland pond also serves to cleanse stormwater on its way to the nearby river. © *Prakash Patel*

Architects often confront competing goals in projects. Hays + Ewing oriented the house parallel to the street grid and created a house that fit well in the neighborhood. The street grid, however, is 28 degrees off south, resulting in primary house views facing south-southwest, a condition that could compromise the passive solar optimization. Consequently, the architects integrated louvers and trellises to provide shading in the summer while allowing the warming light to penetrate the house in the winter. © *Prakash Patel*

The kitchen has the best field of vision anywhere in the house. This vision also encompasses the much used deck and the outdoor play area. Many details were employed to enhance the potential for family interaction. For example, a bar seating area is located on the other side of the kitchen island, providing opportunity for the children and parents to spend time together even while cooking and doing homework. The fiber cement flooring, stained a similar color as a deck, visually connects the indoors to the outdoors. © *Prakash Patel*

Embodying the Japanese spatial concepts of *ma,* or a spatial/temporal distance – the space between that is not nothingness – and *hashi*, or bridging two edges, the glazed bridge serves as a sitting room and connects the public/family spaces to the private master bedroom. A transition zone, it makes a strong connection to the outdoors. It is fully glazed on the two view walls creating a quality of suspension. The other two walls are painted to match the adjacent exterior siding to reinforce the interpenetration of landscape and house.

This space allows for filtered natural light from above with unobstructed views on the ground level. Operable windows throughout the house allow for natural ventilation on both levels. Heart pine and Douglas fir columns and beams, reclaimed from a factory (so that no old growth timber is used), provide the primary structure. Some sustainable strategies are unseen: SIPs provide a superior insulating envelope for the house. Unlike typical stud wall construction with batt insulation, where air penetrations and thermal conductivity at the studs compromise the insulating value of the wall, SIPs provide an optimized thermal wall and roof system. With high-efficiency heating and cooling equipment and passive solar strategies, the house is extremely energy efficient. © *Philip Beaurline*

At the master bath, identical translucent glass doors flank the vanity, one leading to a separate toilet, the other to a shower. To hide a potentially unsightly return duct vent, a custom slatted wood door flanks one side of the sink. An identical door flanks the other side of the vanity and hides the medicine cabinet. © *Prakash Patel*

Creating a dialogue and harmony between architecture and landscape is fundamental to the approach of many architects. Here, the architects collaborated with Nelson Byrd Woltz Landscape Architects, who selected native species for the gardens, resulting in a design that fits well in the Virginia setting. Naturally acclimated, the plants require little or no irrigation and won't adversely affect the habitat, as can non-indigenous species. © *Philip Beaurline*

Deep overhangs shade the house from southern exposure while allowing daylight into the house, thereby reducing energy loads associated with electrical lighting. The southwesterly exposure of the rooms presented a potential for heat gain from the afternoon sun. Working with the daylighting consulting firm Loisos and Ubbelohde, Hays + Ewing developed louvers, seen in the bedroom, that are optimized to occlude direct solar penetration in the summer while allowing the sun to heat the rooms in the winter. Deciduous trees, located on the south of the house, also shade during the summer while allowing the sun to enter the house in the winter. © *Philip Beaurline*

4. LARGE GREEN RESIDENCES

"Where are our castles now, where are our towers?" lamented Sir Thomas More in the late fifteenth century. Although some may insist that green houses should be small houses – and not consume our resources – many Americans still want large houses, but they want them green. Both the National Association of Homebuilders, whose members build a large percentage of the nation's new houses each year, and The Green Building Council penalize much larger homes in the certification process since large homes require more resources. Some of our twenty-first century castles, however, meet those criteria.

The owners of these large new homes often can afford the latest green technologies with their higher up-front costs so they implement them. Some build green-certified mansions, complete with solar heated swimming pools. Others may buy carbon "offsets" for their private jet flights, which help fund alternative energy technologies such as windmills. In this section, we portray green residences over 3,000 square feet built by today's architects.

The two-volume ceiling gives the his/her office space an open airy feel. The abundance of solar-protected and northern exposed glass, open stairways, corridors, and translucent glass provides passive daylight throughout the home. Here, the catwalk-style bridge to the bedrooms adds light through the translucent flooring and subtle illumination. *Courtesy of Taylor Architectural Photography*

The New American Home® 2007

Built as a showcase home for the 2007 International Builders' Show in Orlando, Florida, The New American Home® 2007 illustrates innovative green technologies combined with BSB Design's creative architecture. Because the one-quarter-acre infill lot is adjacent to commercial property and downtown, BSB Design incorporated a modern interpretation of the traditional Craftsman style to bridge the gap between the residential and the urban. Although contemporary in design and function, the 4,300 square-foot home blends seamlessly with the surrounding neighborhood, thanks in large part to its many green elements The house uses 7 percent less energy for heating and cooling and 54 percent less for hot water when compared to a similar home. It is a Certified Florida Green Home by the Florida Green Building Coalition (2007) and Energy Star Certified and follows NAHB Model Green Home Building Guidelines. *Courtesy of JFW Foto*

Energy Star. Energy Star rated appliances and lighting can reduce a home's energy use to a small fraction of the amount consumed by conventionally built homes. The U. S. Environmental Protection Agency (EPA) and the Department of Energy (DOE) run the Energy Star program. Energy Star products use 15- to 75-percent less energy to operate than standard models, meaning you'll save money on your utility bills for as long as you use these products. The Energy Star distinction is available on qualifying products such as furnaces, central and room air conditioners, heat pumps, refrigerators, dishwashers, clothes washers, televisions and VCRs, computers, and even new homes.

Sustainable materials, such as these industrial grade stairs, prevent off-gassing and contribute to the home's durability. Exterior walls are 8-inch precast concrete panels with integrated rigid insulation. A glazing technique adds color and interest without the need for drywall or paint. *Courtesy of Taylor Architectural Photography*

To take advantage of lake views and the downtown skyline, the bottom-up floor plan locates bedrooms on the lower floors and living spaces on the top floor. The extensive master suite features a separate sitting room and a luxurious bath. *Courtesy of JFW Foto*

The custom soaking tub with detailed pebble and tile work sits beneath a "water wall" fountain. A double, glass-enclosed shower provides multiple showerhead configurations and a ceiling-mounted rainfall. *Courtesy of Taylor Architectural Photography*

This kitchen offers restaurant-style finishes, translucent cabinet doors, and deep wood finishes. The massive center island with range is perfect for demonstration cooking and entertaining. *Courtesy of JFW Foto*

The family center extends from the kitchen. Note the open third-floor deck in the background. The windows and the open design connect the home to the outdoors. *Courtesy of Taylor Architectural Photography*

Bioswales. Landscape elements designed to remove silt and pollution from surface runoff water are bioswales. They consist of a swaled drainage course with gently sloped sides (less than six percent) and filled with vegetation, compost and/or riprap.

Four-foot wide planters on each level are vertically aligned to allow filter dripping to the box below. Bioswales, which fill the planters, naturally eliminate impurities from runoff before the water is channeled to the 7,000-gallon cistern. The water is used for irrigation at a rate of 1,200 to 1,500 gal/cycle (1/2 the average), resulting in potable water savings between 208,000 and 260,000 gal/yr. Over 95 percent of all rainwater is kept on site. *Courtesy of JFW Foto*

Outdoor living isn't reserved to the porch and deck. The lap and lounge pool and the pergola-covered patio connect the home to the detached garage; the courtyard provides simple yet beautiful landscaping. *Courtesy of JFW Foto*

The garage has translucent doors to bring in the light. The 7,000-gallon cistern is located beneath the yellow hatch in the center of the floor. *Courtesy of JFW Foto*

The flat green roof, which is accessible through a hatch in the kitchen, features photovoltaic panels and is insulated to R-20 with 300 square feet of natural vegetation. The 2.4-kilowatt photovoltaic system lightens the load by 9-kilowatt hours per day, providing 16 percent of the home's electrical needs. The home utilizes solar power to heat water and supplement the demand for municipal electricity. Two air-source heat pumps, 9.0 HSPF and 17.7 SEER, serve the basement, first, and second floors; a 15 SEER gas/electric unit serves third floor. *Courtesy of JFW Foto*

Seasonal Energy Efficiency Ratio (SEER). The SEER is used to compare central air-conditioning systems as well as heat pumps and add-on heat pumps in their cooling modes. A SEER of 13 or higher is recommended.

Laguna Beach Green

Architect Brion Jeannette designed this elegant yet straightforward home to provide a maximum of passive solar strategies. Site orientation and room relationships follow the solar axis. Window penetrations for daylighting are carefully placed to maximize both light and ventilation. Care has been taken to reduce the glare of harsh light and welcome a gentle natural lighting throughout the 5,500 square-foot house. The home uses sustainable building materials and California native vegetation. *Courtesy of Jeff Kroeze*

Expansive use of double-paned solar tinted glass with optimal exterior overhangs provides maximum natural light while fully operable sidewalls provide maximum ventilation. The thermal mass floors and walls allow for winter heat gain and emphasize the use of sustainable materials. High mass floor materials provide additional heating and cooling retention. *Courtesy of Jeff Kroeze*

The elegant kitchen boasts an entire wall at the built-in table seating area that opens fully to welcome natural ventilation and light. Hydronic radiant floor heating warms the room, and solar panels provide a hot water assist to the tankless water heaters. The kitchen is circled with windows making it easy to use without electrical lighting. High mass floor and counter materials provide additional heating and cooling retention. *Courtesy of Jeff Kroeze*

The entire dual-glazed entry wall of this house faces north, providing the softest form of continual day lighting and visual comfort and allowing cool air to enter the home during warm summer days. *Courtesy of Jeff Kroeze*

Daylighting. Architects increasingly recognize daylighting as an important factor in sustainable design. Approximately 20 percent of the electricity used in the United States is for lighting. When daylighting techniques, such as building and window orientation, placement of windows, other transparent media, and reflective surfaces, exterior shading, clerestory windows, and skylights are used appropriately, natural light can provide sufficient internal illumination during the day. A passive solar method of using sunlight to provide illumination, daylighting can directly offset energy use in electric lighting systems and indirectly offset energy use through a reduction in cooling load.

The entire dual glazed entry wall extends the full two levels. Skylights and west-facing glass walls augment the lighting. *Courtesy of Jeff Kroeze*

The master bedroom on the second level enjoys full view of the Pacific Ocean with minimal heat gain. Sidewalls with large operable glazing systems provide natural ventilation. The Lutron Homeworks Interactive lighting system throughout the house coupled with the recessed cove lighting allows for reduced lighting output and gentle illumination with reduced energy consumption. *Courtesy of Jeff Kroeze*

A gentle curving wall that surrounds the tub separates the master bathroom and bedroom. Solar panels provide heating for domestic hot water, and plumbing fixtures are water saving. As in the kitchen, high thermal mass floors and counters augment the heating and cooling systems. The hydronic radiant floor heating keeps the bathroom warm in winter. Assisted by tankless water heaters, solar panels heat domestic hot water and the pool. *Courtesy of Jeff Kroeze*

This home enjoys a year-round pool. In the summer months, the glass walls are pushed within the stone support walls to reveal continual access to the exterior patio. In winter, the glass walls provide protection from the elements. *Courtesy of Jeff Kroeze*

Matoaka

Carter + Burton Architecture designed this Virginia home (built by Jon Duval) to stretch out along the east-west axis, taking advantage of passive solar strategies on the southern elevation and the panoramic views to the valley. The slope of the modified shed roof relates to the surrounding natural area: low horizontal lines mimic the plane of the grasses, and the edge of the higher shed roof is aligned with the existing tree line. The exterior materials of stucco, timber, and copper create a low maintenance, regional response to the surrounding agrarian setting. *Courtesy of Jim Burton*

The open risers of this locally crafted stair tower at the core of the house link views through spaces both vertically and horizontally while allowing natural light to pass through all the way down to the basement. The open stairs provide flexibility, light, ventilation, and the appearance of extra space. The concrete floor from the living room hallway wraps around the corner of the core. *Courtesy of Daniel Azfal*

This modern country kitchen allows household members to stay connected during food preparation. The built-in benches in the corner provide an informal breakfast area with game and blanket storage under the seating. The passive solar design placed all of the cabinets below the countertop using dish drawers for storage below. The large overhangs warm the countertops in the winter and shade them in the summer. The pantry core creates a shift in the circulation axis and provides ample storage including a butler's pantry, connecting the kitchen to the formal dining space. High north windows above the pantry provide balanced daylighting, and the wood ceiling provides warmth while bringing the scale of the space down for a more cozy setting. *Courtesy of Daniel Azfal*

Highlighting the client's interest in Japanese architecture, the "solar engawa" serves as a connection piece in multiple ways. This interior concrete circulation path links the kitchen and hall to the main living space and extends to the master bedroom. The southern sun warms the concrete floor, which, in turn, passively warms the living room. The glass of the sliding doors also blends the inside hallway with the outside terrace and views of the Blue Ridge Mountains beyond. The cantilevered shading louvers provide solar protection in the summer months and bring the scale down at the engawa layer. *Courtesy of Daniel Azfal*

The client's love of Frank Lloyd Wright and Japanese design inspired this family gathering place around the hearth. The fireplace represents the integration of art as architecture, showcasing the warmth of materials used in sustainable design. The concrete and stone chimney mass support structural elements as well as return ducts and the chimney. Sustainable materials such as glue-lam beams, SIPs roof and wall panels, bamboo floors, and an exposed concrete core revolve around this hearth made of stone reused from a local farmhouse destroyed by fire. *Courtesy of Daniel Azfal*

CARLIN HILL

Architect George Fellner decided to build a New England shingle-style farmhouse hybrid that had sustainable design attributes. This view shows the 3,240 square-foot house with a walkout basement. Fellner used the large boulders excavated from the site to form retaining walls. The sunroom at the right side acts as a counterpoint to the main gable form. Fellner designed the window placement to provide maximum natural ventilation throughout the house. *Photo by George Fellner*

The Fellners participated in the Northeast Utilities Energy Star Program, with a conscious effort to integrate plan orientation, window placement, envelope efficiency, natural ventilation, and passive solar heating so to optimize sustainability. A major component is the GeoExchange heating and cooling system, including two 300-feet deep closed-loop wells and a 5-ton geothermal heat pump. They found this participation to be most cost-effective. The geothermal wells are set in the foreground and are not visible from above. The below-ground connection enters the basement at the northwest corner of the house. *Photo by George Fellner*

The intersecting and shifting gable-hip roof forms and the projecting bays created an eastern entry garden-courtyard, as well as multiple, intimate spaces. *Photo by George Fellner*

This interior view shows the bluestone-faced, high efficiency, closed combustion fireplace, which helps heat the house as well as providing ambiance. The cathedral ceiling is structured from a salvaged 200-year old lumber tie-beam/brace. The interior detailing incorporates simple stained pine trim, which is constant throughout the house. The French doors lead into the sunroom. *Photo by Jerry Reed*

99

This passive solar space with stock windows, skylights, and bluestone floor offers a welcome retreat for soaking in the spa tub. *Photo by Jerry Reed*

This informal space also has the salvaged 200-year-old lumber tie-beam/brace system. The built-out soffits contain ductwork from the geothermal system. *Photo by Jerry Reed*

This twilight view of the house reveals the interior tie-beam/brace system, repeated by the exterior second floor truss work. *Photo by George Fellner*

Westview Residence

This 3,256 square-foot residence designed by Barley & Pfeiffer Architects received a Five Star (certified) rating by the Austin Green Building Program and was selected for the 2005 Cool Homes Tour in West Austin. It is one of the few Five-Star rated homes in the area.

Its features include stained concrete, natural wood and cork floors, hydronic heating, energy-efficient air conditioning with cooling tower, spray foam insulation, enhanced daylighting and natural ventilation, Energy Star appliances, and energy-efficient Marvin windows.

Barley & Pfeiffer oriented all major windows so to capture prevailing breezes and aid in solar shading while allowing for natural illumination and winter heating from the sun. The windows have a minimum of 36-inch overhangs and were accurately sized for optimum solar shading. Operable windows high up in the stair tower provide for ample natural ventilation and balance out the natural daylighting of this home. Mechanically operated windows located in the stair tower vent the air inside the home. Ground floor windows draw in cooler air as the hot air exits the house. © *Connie Moberly*

Cooling Tower. A cooling tower is a heat rejection device, which expels waste heat to the atmosphere though the cooling of a water stream to a lower temperature. In the house designed by Hubbell & Hubbell, a cooling tower with a fan and windows cools in the summer by drawing out hot air and re-circulates warm air in the winter. *Courtesy of Drew Hubbell*

The energy reduction strategy is aimed to reduce heat gain in this Texan home. The metal roof contains a self-venting radiant barrier system, which keeps attic temperatures close to that of the outside – 40 degrees cooler than a typical attic in the area. Insulation board installed under the upstairs ceiling provides a thermal break between the finished ceiling and the roof structure, keeping upper floors more comfortable in the summer months. © *Connie Moberly*

The screened porch is strategically placed to capture southeasterly breezes. Like many of the rooms in the house, it has a ceiling fan. Its floor is stained concrete. © *Connie Moberly*

The client and the landscape designer made extensive use of low water-use vegetation. The site debris was chipped and used as mulch while the existing topsoil was harvested and stored on site for use during final grading. The metal used in the roofing is made from post-industrial recycled steel. A special heavy-duty building wrap protects the house framing from mold and wood decay while reducing the work the air conditioner has to do in the summer to de-humidify the home. © *Connie Moberly*

The walls are insulated with a special "wet blown" cellulose fill that blocks even the smallest possible source of heat loss – much more effectively than standard fiberglass batts. Composed of recycled cardboard, this less toxic fill contributes to a more healthful indoor air quality. The insulation also contains a harmless boric acid powder that effectively stops pests while not introducing potentially dangerous chemicals. © *Connie Moberly*

Instead of the conventional condensing units usually found on most residential air-conditioning systems, a small cooling tower employs evaporative cooling to improve efficiency. The air handling system provides a slight positive pressure to this home's interior, further reducing the possibility of humid outside air in the summer and annoying cold drafts in the winter infiltrating the home. © *Connie Moberly*

Big Dig House

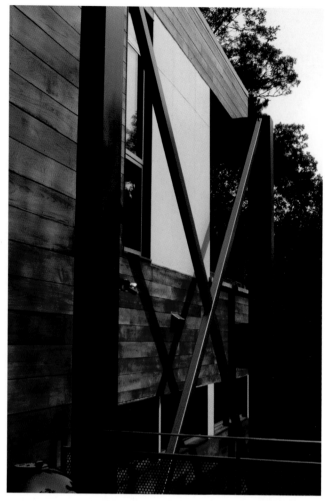

Constructed from 600,000 pounds of recycled materials, the three-story house is built to stand forever. It took only two days and a massive crane to frame the house. Other than the concrete foundations, the concrete block garage wing, and the cross beam originally thought necessary for bracing, the exterior is mostly glass and cedar siding, softened by an elaborate roof garden atop the garage. *Courtesy of D. Peter Lund*

Good green architecture reduces the waste of energy and material. Using recycled materials in constructing a house represents an important advance in sustainable building; utilizing waste from building projects is another significant step in developing a sustainable building industry. Not only does reusing waste from construction projects reduce the burden on our landfills, it conserves our natural resources and can lower construction costs.

Paul Pedini's firm was one of the principal contractors for Boston's Big Dig, one of the nation's largest highway projects. Over a 15-year period, this multi-billion-dollar project rerouted highways through the center of Boston, replacing them with a 3.5-mile tunnel. The project required thousands of tons of steel, hardware and prefabricated reinforced-concrete slabs, 10 feet wide and up to 80 feet long, to build temporary ramps and roadways. At the project's end, the Commonwealth of Massachusetts planned to pay to take the materials to the landfill, where they would be buried. A civil engineer with vision, Pedini realized that these materials could be salvaged, saving the nation's landfill space, resources, and taxpayer dollars.

Pedini returned the money to the Commonwealth, which, in turn, gave him the highway panels and bridge piers. First, he used them for another project, and then he used 13 of these 23,000-pound slabs to build his stunning 4,300-square-foot home. *Courtesy of D. Peter Lund*

Once part of an elevated expressway, these monolithic panels with their imbedded steel beams are now the floors and ceilings of the Big Dig House. Highway beams are dramatic vertical and horizontal supports for these slabs of concrete roadway decking. *Courtesy of D. Peter Lund*

The height of the house allows good daylight and views of the woods surrounding the house. Rather than paving a large area for a circular driveway, the design called for the garage to be a drive-through! *Courtesy of D. Peter Lund*

Recycled/Reused Building Materials. Architectural salvage (e. g., cast iron artifacts, marble mantels, stained glass) has always been popular. Today, many cities have "reuse" stores, which sell salvaged goods — from electric fixtures to used floorboards — for 50 to 75 percent off what similar products would cost if purchased new. The Building Materials Reuse Association (BMRA) is a non-profit educational organization whose mission is to facilitate building deconstruction and the reuse/recycling of recovered building materials. Its website displays a current listing of these stores nationwide.

The 27-inch-wide painted girder (that once helped prop up slurry walls along Boston's Storrow Drive) now helps support the home's 69,000-pound roof. The surrounding fence is salvaged from a local demolition project. *Courtesy of D. Peter Lund*

The acid-treated concrete floors resemble modern oils and contain energy-efficient radiant heating. A towering bank of windows emits light in the Great Room, which can be warmed by the basaltic stone fireplace when necessary. The stovepipe that soars to the ceiling echoes the verticality of the windows. *Courtesy of D. Peter Lund*

If you follow the stovepipe up, you see the date when the panel was cast on the ceiling panel. *Courtesy of D. Peter Lund*

In the kitchen/dining area, a long steel beam runs along the ceiling. *Courtesy of D. Peter Lund*

Other sustainable features are the roof garden that serves as an outdoor patio above the garage and a rainwater retrieval system for irrigation. Excess water is drained into a garage cistern. Steel forms once used to make precast beams act as planters. A pair of Chinese foo dogs guards the doors of this Asian garden. *Courtesy of D. Peter Lund*

Situated on a ridge, this 3,200 square-foot house commands a 270-degree view of the Pacific Ocean, a dramatic canyon, and the Santa Inez mountains. Although not immediately obvious, Shubin + Donaldson Architects' design embraces several characteristics of environmentally sustainable design. The site of the house is based on solar orientation, resulting in passive solar gains throughout the year. Photovoltaic power generates household electricity through a 2.8-kilowatt system; when power is not needed, it feeds back into the grid. A passive rooftop solar heating system provides for domestic hot water, and a passive solar ground-level hot water system heats the pool. *Courtesy of Ciro Coelho Photography*

A dramatic glass canopy ceremoniously marks the entrance. It, like the deep exterior overhangs, provides shade in the summer and lets in sun during the winter. Other energy-saving systems include double-pane windows, UV-resistant glass, ample insulation, and energy-efficient appliances. *Courtesy of Ciro Coelho Photography*

Floor-to-ceiling bookshelves complement the mahogany living room wall that houses an entertainment center. Set into the wall, and surrounded by floor-to-ceiling glass, it acts as an extension of the outdoors. *Courtesy of Ciro Coelho Photography*

The neutral color scheme complements the colors of nature that comprise the predominant palette. *Courtesy of Ciro Coelho Photography*

The natural flow of hot and cool air is fortified by the use of radiant hot water floor heating and separate central air conditioning in the ceilings. Although these systems are in place, they are rarely used because of the solar orientation of the home and the natural ventilation. *Courtesy of Ciro Coelho Photography*

The amply insulated kitchen, complete with energy-efficient appliances, faces the hillside. Shubin + Donaldson Architects re-used the existing foundation and caissons. During construction, the existing house was taken apart piece-by-piece, and all usable elements were donated to Habitat for Humanity. *Courtesy of Ciro Coelho Photography*

Doorways in general – even in the limestone-clad bathrooms – are taller than usual and lead the eye upward to be rewarded by either natural light or a beautiful vista. *Courtesy of Ciro Coelho Photography*

The stunning natural light saves energy throughout the house. Four separate terraces surround the house, continuing the indoor/outdoor feeling and accessibility. *Courtesy of Ciro Coelho Photography*

Heated by a passive solar ground-level hot water system, the infinity pool just outside the living room leads the eye to the ocean and the Channel Islands beyond. Four separate terraces surround the house, continuing the indoor/outdoor feeling and accessibility. *Courtesy of Ciro Coelho Photography*

Throughout the house, the walls intersect with glass in a play of solidity and transparency. *Courtesy of Ciro Coelho Photography*

Whistling Winds

Whistling Winds, which features a variety of off-the-shelf, sustainable materials, was one of BSB Design's first custom homes to utilize green technologies on a large scale. This contemporary red farmhouse is neatly tucked away in dense Florida vegetation. Photovoltaic panels (creatively positioned as awnings over the garage doors) supplement the home's electrical consumption. The home is currently in the process of obtaining green certification from the Florida Green Building Coalition. © *Everett & Soulé*

Visible ductwork and concrete block are not typical custom home finishes, but green concepts embrace such minimalism and use it as a design advantage. © *Everett & Soulé*

The industrial feel of exposed beams and concrete floor in the family center is juxtaposed with warm sunshine and comfortable furnishings. © *Everett & Soulé*

An open joist system supports the second floor, another "off-the-shelf" concept that requires no elaborate finishing yet still creates architectural interest. © *Everett & Soulé*

This office, with wonderful views of the surrounding woodlands, includes a "nest" accessible through wall cut-outs and a small stair – another way green design makes efficient use of otherwise wasted space. © *Everett & Soulé*

Green design is all about efficiency – and connections to the natural environment. The outer wall of the master bath private patio has been outfitted with simple wire fencing used as a trellis – another "off-the-shelf" concept with a very pleasing result. The windmill pays homage to more self-sustaining times, given the agricultural background of the location. © *Everett & Soulé*

The industrial stair is a great example of sustainable design. Heavy duty and nearly maintenance-free, it will last a long time. © *Everett & Soulé*

The green movement is also an attempt to reconnect us to our environment. This private walled patio extends from the master bathroom through a large sliding glass door in the shower. A hot shower (complete with waterfall showerheads) in the cool morning breeze can help provide that ultimate spa-like experience © *Everett & Soulé*

Toronto House

Designed and built as a personal residence by Altius for one of the partners, this house exemplifies the firm's design philosophy and is a showcase of integrated sustainable technology. Located just steps from Toronto's bustling Bloor West Village, the 5,300 square-foot residence is buried into the steep wooded slope. The combination of earth sheltering, correct solar geometry, and extremely tight building envelope is the residence's first line of defense against the elements. *Courtesy of Altius/Paterson*

The driveway utilizes porous brick pavers while the rest of the property is planted with native perennial plantings requiring minimal irrigation. The exterior sandstone walls were salvaged from a local home that was demolished. Durable natural materials such as harvested ipe decking and copper with high recycled content improve with age and give the project a distinctive patina. *Courtesy of Altius/Paterson*

A three-story high stair well extends up the back wall of the house. Windows at the bottom of the stair and operable skylights up top create a thermal siphon at night to vent the house and dump heat from the brick.

Every space in the home is accessed by natural daylight. The sun moves through the home creating wonderfully dramatic moments. The wall is faced in yellow clay brick that provides tremendous thermal mass. The heavy timber frame and decking is harvested Douglas fir; half of the timbers were salvaged from a WWII aircraft hanger outside of Ottawa. *Courtesy of Altius/Paterson*

In Toronto, cooling is just as important as heating as seasonal temperatures range from 100°F down to -20°F. Extremely efficient double low-E windows are used to keep heat in and provide substantial solar gain in the winter. All of the materials and finishes in the house are inert and free of volatile organic compounds. A separate air handling system filters the air and provides fresh air and supplemental humidity in wintertime. The concrete floors and brick walls absorb the heat and maintain stable indoor temperatures. *Courtesy of Altius/Paterson*

The main living space on the third level enjoys an open Rumford fireplace and a Finnish masonry stove. The chimneys are internalized with chimney top dampers to retain all the heat that builds up in the masonry mass. Exterior air is vented into the fire chambers to ensure clean and complete wood combustion. Polished concrete floors contain radiant hydronic heating loops that are fed by a geothermal heat pump. *Courtesy of Altius/Paterson*

Although the city is at the doorstep of this lovely home, the views from the main living spaces are carefully composed to highlight the greenery that surrounds the house. *Courtesy of Altius/Paterson*

The roof terrace off the main living space on the third level provides privacy while offering an opportunity to interact with neighbors and passers-by on the street below. A band of green roof with up to 10 inches of soil is planted with native species and catches rainwater run-off from the deck. The green roof is very effective at preventing summer heat gain and providing evaporative cooling and storm water retention. *Courtesy of Altius/Paterson*

Green Roofs or Roof Gardens. A roof can be turned into a cultivated area or a green roof. Not only does a green roof combat temperature variations, but it also leads to better sun and thermal insulation. It also improves the surrounding microclimate by absorbing dust and pollutants, cooling the roof surface, and retaining more rainwater, thus reducing run off. *Courtesy of Wolbrink Architects*

California Sushi

An early pioneer in solar design, Architect David Wright designed this 4,400 square-foot modern adaptation of Japanese style in the Sierra Nevada Mountains of California. The house, which uses SIPs, is much like the traditional Japanese tatami module. *Courtesy of Steve Solinsky*

Within one dwelling, a number of micro-climate zones are created: sun and shade porches, screened porch room, basement cool zones, and passive solar great room. *Courtesy of Steve Solinsky*

The native slate-surfaced, radiant heated concrete floors provide solar thermal mass and efficient heat distribution throughout the house. The liquefied petroleum gas high efficiency boiler provides even efficient warm floors throughout as well as domestic hot water back up. *Courtesy of Steve Solinsky*

Native wood, such as locally produced Douglas fir, cedar and pine lumber, florescent lights, and high-efficiency appliances are used throughout. *Courtesy of Steve Solinsky*

The efficient windows are insulated glass wood frame windows with low-E glazing on east, west, and north sides. Ceilings fans keep the interior air flowing in both summer and winter. *Courtesy of Steve Solinsky*

The south-facing glass maximizes winter sun gain. High venting skylights allow warm air to escape, bringing in fresh air in from any direction below. The grid inter-tied solar electric panels (photovoltaic) offset the entire electrical load. The traditional clay Japanese roof tiles provide natural cooling and aesthetics. *Courtesy of Steve Solinsky*

Green New England Colonial

This classic New England colonial, designed and constructed by Barry Katz Homebuilding, Inc., is green mostly in ways that are not immediately apparent to the casual observer. Although the vast majority of green homes that get published seem to be in a contemporary idiom and often include innovative or unconventional design features, very little about building green actually dictates architectural style. Katz set out to create a home that would evoke the sensibilities of an earlier era but was nonetheless very green.

Note the classic red-painted garage, for example. It is all but separate from the main body of the house in order to prevent unwanted fumes from degrading the home's pristine indoor air quality. The Home Builders Association of Connecticut awarded it the 2007 HOBI (Home Building Industry) Award for "Best Green House." *Courtesy of Barry Katz Homebuilding, Inc.*

To conserve natural resources, the home's structure employs engineered lumber made from small diameter, fast-growing trees. These materials provide greater structural integrity and dimensional stability than sawn lumber without placing a strain on old-growth forests. The columns are made from fiber cement composite for durability and resource conservation.

The interior blends classical detailing with sustainable technologies. Programmable thermostats, like the one visible to the right of the living room's Doric columns, help reduce energy use. The flooring is made from bamboo, another rapidly renewable resource. *Courtesy of Barry Katz Homebuilding, Inc.*

Sprayed foam insulation and high-performance windows with argon filled low-E glass create a tight thermal envelope that minimizes the home's heating and cooling needs. Roofing shingles that deflect the sun's heat further reduce cooling loads in summer. A super-efficient geothermal system that burns no fossil fuel and emits no C02 provides heating and cooling. It is coupled with energy recovery ventilation units (ERVs) and electrostatic air cleaners for optimal indoor air quality. *Courtesy of Barry Katz Homebuilding, Inc.*

Insulation. A well-insulated building envelope is essential in the design of an environmentally sound building. When heat transfer through the building envelope is reduced, energy used to maintain the interior climate is also decreased, thereby saving both energy and environmental costs.

Fiberglass batts are commonly used for insulating walls and ceilings. Cellulose insulation is made from recycled paper that is applied as either loose fill into attics and closed wall cavities or damp-sprayed into open wall cavities. Because of its recycled content and potentially higher energy and acoustic performance, cellulose is an environmentally preferable product. *Courtesy of Wolbrink Architects*

In this house designed by Barry Katz Homebuilding, even the unfinished attic spaces are insulated with BioBased foam made from soybeans. Sprayed foam provides high R-values while completely eliminating air leaks, the major cause of heat loss. Placing ductwork and air handlers within insulated spaces helps to maximize energy efficiency. *Courtesy of Barry Katz Homebuilding, Inc.*

All light fixtures in the home, including the dining room sconces seen here, use compact fluorescent light bulbs (CFLs) with a color temperature of 2,700 K, which mimics the warm appearance of incandescent light. CFLs use one fourth as much electricity as incandescent bulbs and produce much less heat. *Courtesy of Barry Katz Homebuilding, Inc.*

Compact Fluorescent Lamps (CFLs). Energy Star qualified CFLs use about 75 percent less energy than standard incandescent bulbs and last up to 10 times longer. They also save about $30 or more in electricity costs over each bulb's lifetime and produce about 75 percent less heat, so they're safer to operate and can cut energy costs associated with home cooling. Energy Star recommends installing qualified CFLs in fixtures that are used at least 15 minutes at a time or several hours per day. They are available in different sizes and shapes to fit in almost any fixture, for indoors and outdoors.

Energy Recovery Ventilator. Ventilation is crucial in tightly constructed houses. Seen in the house designed by Barry Katz Homebuilding, this energy recovery ventilator provides a constant supply of fresh air while conserving thermal energy and keeping humidity levels balanced. *Courtesy of Barry Katz Homebuilding, Inc.*

A special non-toxic adhesive was used to lay the mudroom's cork flooring, another rapidly renewable resource. All the interior paints and finishes contain zero VOC, and indoor air quality is further enhanced by construction techniques that control humidity, while electrostatic air cleaners remove dust, pollen, mold spores, and even most bacteria and viruses. *Courtesy of Barry Katz Homebuilding, Inc.*

A traditional butler's pantry provides extra storage and doubles as a home office. It is fitted out with compartments for computer equipment to facilitate telecommuting. In the kitchen, as throughout the house, the custom cabinetry is made from formaldehyde-free plywood to ensure healthy indoor air quality. Energy Star rated appliances and lighting conserve energy. *Courtesy of Barry Katz Homebuilding, Inc.*

The luxurious master bath features a heated marble floor, which enables homeowners to feel comfortable without raising the thermostat. Dual-flush toilets and a hot water recirculation system activated by motion sensors conserve thousands of gallons of water per year. *Courtesy of Barry Katz Homebuilding, Inc.*

Dual Flush Toilets. The average person flushes five times per day, and four of those are for liquids. Dual-flush technology offers a choice of two water levels – one for each type of waste. A dual-flush toilet resembles any other toilet, except that the user chooses one of two buttons, depending on the type of waste.

Not only do these toilets save water, they are highly efficient. The 1.6-gallon setting will consistently remove bulk waste with just one flush, eliminating the need for double flushing.

A recent study showed that dual-flush toilets could reduce the amount of water used in a single-family residence by 68 percent; they reduced the water used in office bathrooms by 56 percent. For septic tank users, dual-flush toilets can reduce system loads up to 72 percent. *Courtesy of Wolbrink Architects*

40 Percent Less Energy

Oz Architecture designed this residence to use 40 percent less energy than a code-compliant standard home in the Denver area. ENSAR Group performed energy analysis on the design and provided recommendations with regards to materials, renewable technology possibilities, and energy performance. The energy modeling used was ENERGY-10, an hourly simulation program developed at the National Renewable Energy Laboratory.

The exterior of the house is constructed with SIPs with an R-24 insulation value, locally quarried 4-inch Colorado Buff stone veneer, and three-coat cement stucco for the exterior wall finishes. The roof is a curved standing seam metal roof with a durable bronze kynar finish. *Courtesy of Ron Ruscio Photography*

The properly sized windows and roof overhangs facing south provide efficient solar gain in the winter and shade in the summer. The operable lower windows on the south side allow for natural nighttime ventilation. The colored concrete floor absorbs the winter sunrays, and the large vaulted ceilings allow for any excess heat to rise to the upper rooms to the north. *Courtesy of Ron Ruscio Photography*

The kitchen floor is manufactured from palm trees that no longer produce fruit. The high efficiency gas boiler produces domestic hot water. *Courtesy of Ron Ruscio Photography*

The master bath has durable stone tile with radiant in-floor heating. The granite stone tub is fabricated within a 500-mile radius. *Courtesy of Ron Ruscio Photography*

The nursery has a south-facing clerestory with a deep light shelf to keep direct solar gain but maintain indirect day lighting into the room. *Courtesy of Ron Ruscio Photography*

126

Spicewood Residence

Miguel Rivera of Mira Rivera Architects designed this 5,113 square-foot house, which is divided into a main residence with a large kitchen at its core and a guesthouse. The principal views are oriented towards the north, the view to the lake. As the house rises upward, the walls become more open, culminating in a 360-degree view office at the third level and an observation tower at the fourth level. *Courtesy of Jenee Arthur*

The exterior materials were selected to reflect the Texas Hill landscape: Arkansas calico limestone, light painted stucco, and galvalume roofing. This simple palette unfolds in striking manner. The stone and stucco are coursed in strong horizontal bands, while the metal roofing folds into oversized gutters. Cypress wood stretches in a continuous plane from the 8-foot soffit overhangs to the second floor ceilings. The same material wraps down the staircase and up to the third floor office and fourth level observation deck. *Courtesy of Jenee Arthur*

The owners wanted low electric bills, which led to this sustainable design. The house is oriented with its long sides to the north and south, with the majority of the glazing on the north. Deep overhangs protect the facade. *Courtesy of Jenee Arthur*

The pool terrace between the house and guesthouse provides a welcome place to catch the prevailing winds. *Courtesy of Jenee Arthur*

The house can run entirely on rainwater that is collected from the barn roof into 20,000-gallon cisterns. *Courtesy of Jenee Arthur*

The cypress and glass door reinforces the horizontal motifs of the house design and ties into the wood soffits 20 feet above. *Courtesy of Jenee Arthur*

The mechanical system uses geothermal coils to displace heat into the ground, eliminating the need for noisy condensing units while conserving electricity use. These features allowed the house to earn a strong 3-star rating with the Austin Green Building Program.

Prairie Concept Development House

The three-acre lot has a long dramatic approach, great views, privacy, and sloping grade toward an adjacent pond. The northwest elevation of this Indiana green house designed by Perkins VonDeylen Architects features a main level covered terrace, which blends into the site through landscape walls, native boulders, walkways, and plantings that connect to the house again at the basement walkout. *Courtesy of Perkins VonDeylen Architects*

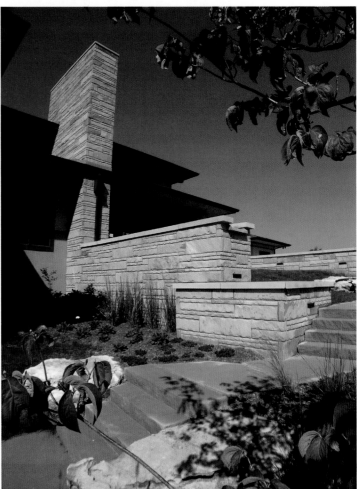

In this residence, rain turns into a celebrated event when it collects from the roof and runs along a trough on the top of this landscape wall. At the end of the run, it drops several feet as a garden waterfall, and then collects in a cistern to be used later for irrigation. The landscape elements also include indigenous, drought-tolerant, low-maintenance prairie plantings. *Courtesy of Perkins VonDeylen Architects*

The exterior walls are a hybrid of insulated concrete forms and stick framing insulated and sealed with non-toxic sprayed-on polyurethane foam. Lending itself to the Prairie style, the broad roof overhangs also help to shade high summer sun angles and shield the exterior finish against harsher weather.
Courtesy of Perkins VonDeylen Architects

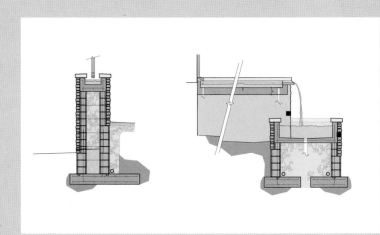

Rooftop Catchment Systems. Rainwater harvesting has been practiced for over 4,000 years. As can be seen here, a rainwater harvesting system consists of three basic elements: a collection area, a conveyance system, and storage facilities. The collection area in most cases is the roof of a house or a building. The effective roof area and the material used in constructing the roof influence the efficiency of collection and the water quality.

Gutters or pipes deliver rainwater falling on the rooftop to cisterns or other storage vessels. Rainwater collectors are used for similar purposes. In some areas, homes use specially designed rainwater collectors to gather rainwater for all water use, including drinking water.
Courtesy of Perkins VonDeylen Architects

Landscape walls with a local sandstone veneer visually connect the house to its setting. Here, the landscape wall divides the formal from the informal entry and draws the eye into the cantilever covered porch. Double-paned, insulated, low-E coated windows are complemented with art glass in the stair tower fenestration. *Courtesy of Perkins VonDeylen Architects*

The core living area has high clerestory windows that provide ample, indirect natural daylighting. A dual fuel furnace provides heating; a "smart home system" controls light and sound centrally. *Courtesy of Perkins VonDeylen Architects*

The interior wood trim is made of locally harvested poplar stained to match the cherry cabinetry. *Courtesy of Perkins VonDeylen Architects*

Much of the main level floor is made from highly renewable bamboo. The bamboo also climbs the stair steps, where the Craftsman style railing made of locally harvested poplar complements it. *Courtesy of Perkins VonDeylen Architects*

Su Hacienda Ideal

This light and colorful home designed by Barley & Pfeiffer achieves superior energy efficiency and indoor air quality by means of thoughtful design and choice of materials, as well as careful consideration of health and safety issues. © *Connie Moberly*

The well-oriented house has enhanced natural ventilation and daylighting. The roof and walls employ a radiant barrier strategy to reduce heat gain. A special heavy duty building wrap controls outdoor air infiltration, protecting the home from mold, wood decay, and outside pollutants, while helping to reduce the air conditioning load. An integrated pest management system is employed. The mechanical system is rated at SEER 14 minimum, and all metal ductwork is insulated and properly sealed to ensure energy efficiency. All this efficiency is concealed in a delightful hacienda-style space that delights its owners with shifting color, richness of material, and changing quality of light throughout the day. © *Connie Moberly*

The metal roof contains a self-venting radiant barrier system, which consists of dual venting paths. The underside of the roof decking is sprayed with icynene spray foam insulation. This water-based formula, which contains no formaldehyde, CFCs, or HCFCs, seals the attic, making it part of the thermal envelope. Incidentally, the metal used in the roofing is made from post-industrial recycled steel. © *Connie Moberly*

All living areas and bedrooms have ceiling fans. A minimum of 36-inch window and roof overhangs provide summer shading, yet allow for ample natural lighting and passive solar heating from the sun. All windows have had sun angle calculations performed on them. © *Connie Moberly*

The house has a zoned, 14 SEER air conditioning system with programmable thermostats. This system results in greater comfort control, less energy consumption, and greater flexibility as the living needs change over time.

The air handling system provides a slight positive pressure to the home's interior, further reducing the possibility of humid and pollen-laden outside air or cold winter drafts. The duct system is constructed of sealed sheet metal, maximizing even airflow throughout the house and reducing the chance of some rooms being warmer, or cooler, than others. This attention to detail also reduces the chance for dirt or molds to accumulate inside the ducts and duct leakage, a major source of energy waste in most homes. © *Connie Moberly*

The house contains many low toxicity materials: spray foam insulation, termi-mesh termite treatment, boric acid pest control, stained, exposed concrete floors, and an engineered mesquite wood flooring with a water-based polyurethane finish (instead of mold-trapping carpet). © *Connie Moberly*

Courtyard House

Located in a neighborhood characterized by traditional single-family residences, this 3,917 square-foot house designed by VaST sets a new benchmark for a contemporary, energy-efficient and environmentally sensitive design in the Denver area. *Courtesy of Erik Paulsrud*

Reclaimed cedar siding, durable stucco, and natural stone tile compose the "green" exterior pallet. Exterior walls and roof are built with locally made, fire- and mold-resistant SIPs, which provide an extremely energy-efficient and airtight building envelope while minimizing the use of materials. Nominally, the walls are insulated to R28 and the roof to R42, but effectively the performance is much higher when compared with typical "stick-framed" walls and roofs insulated with conventional fiberglass batts. *Courtesy of Erik Paulsrud*

The concrete floors made with 20-percent fly ash have in-floor radiant heat. Concrete, stone, and tile floors provide thermal mass which helps regulate the temperature of a home. Thermal mass provides great comfort by retaining heat in the winter and remaining cool in the summer. The polished concrete floors have the additional benefit of being long-lasting and low maintenance while avoiding any toxic off-gassing commonly associated with carpeting. *Courtesy of Erik Paulsrud*

Stair treads are made from laminated pine beam (Glu-Lam®). Finger-joint lumber (made by joining shorter pieces of wood together) was used to frame the interior. Indoor air quality was a major concern. The heat recovery ventilation (HRV) system provides pre-heated fresh air in the winter months. No VOC paint was used throughout. The polished concrete flooring helps reduce dust and dander build-up associated with carpet. *Courtesy of Erik Paulsrud*

European style cabinetry contains less urea-formaldehyde than American cabinetry. *Courtesy of Erik Paulsrud*

VaST employed passive solar design techniques to increase solar heat gain during winter days and reduce gain in the summer. South-facing glazing allows for passive solar heating in the winter months; the overhangs help keep unwanted sun out in the summer. *Courtesy of Erik Paulsrud*

The thoughtful design obscures the photovoltaic (solar electric) panels from street-view. The 3.75-kilowatt array generates 50 percent of the home's electric needs. The use of irrigation water was minimized by the landscaping design. *Courtesy of Erik Paulsrud*

Shenandoah Retreat House

Carter + Burton Architecture points out that the concept of "green design" does not need to be separated from "good design." Sustainable design principles are a part of the poetics of their design through the blending of old and new technologies such as concrete and wood with SIPs, steel, and glass. Each material performs the way it is meant to in this minimalist expression of sustainable design principles. *Courtesy of Daniel Afzal*

The deck wrapping the western side of the house links to the lower terrace and chemical-free spa with intermediate nodes, which includes the summer kitchen and eat-in screened porch. The butterfly roof controls sun and water from affecting the interior of the house. *Courtesy of Daniel Afzal*

Minimal furnishings are aided by custom built-in storage along the north wall. The high cool north light mixes with the warm southern light for balanced daylighting. The fireplace is made from Heatcrete, a more durable material suitable for high temperatures. *Courtesy of Daniel Afzal*

The owner wished to provide a minimalist foreground in which to enjoy nature through the windows beyond. The inhabitant becomes directly engaged with the view at the built-in dining table and benches made from stabilized aluminum foam (100-percent recyclable and non-combustible). The exposed concrete floor and cantilevered concrete office balcony warm in the winter sun and slowly release this heat in the evenings. This radiant heat is critical to energy efficiency as it keeps the heat down low where the furniture and people are, rather than warming the air, which will rise to the high ceiling. *Courtesy of Daniel Afzal*

The master bedroom of this critically acclaimed modern home provides the owner with a tree house experience by raising the bed into the height of the tree branches. The windows of the master bedroom extend into nature as a passive solar bay. *Courtesy of Daniel Afzal*

The tall mass of the Carter + Burton Architecture retreat house blends in with the surrounding trees and frames views of the site while forming exterior spaces between the volumes. A floating formal entrance separates the private bedroom wing from the public living wing. The concrete tower highlighted in the center of the house, reminiscent of fire lookouts in the surrounding mountains, serves as an exhaust for rising hot air in the summer through operable windows. The SIP roof panels provide an elegant profile. The exterior grill center and screen porch are essential in keeping extra heat out of the house in Virginia's hot, humid summers. *Courtesy of Daniel Afzal*

Spanish Mission Eco Style

Hubbell & Hubbell designed a post and frame house with straw bale infill around a massive boulder that helps provide an energy rating exceeding California's compliance standard by 41 percent. Straw is inexpensive, clean, and lightweight; it also provides such advantages as energy efficiency and resistance to seismic stresses. The super-insulated straw bale walls make the building act like a thermos that holds in heat during the winter and cool air during the summer. Solar panels heat the water, and future photovoltaic panels in conjunction with existing inverter and battery storage will eventually provide most of the home's electricity. *Courtesy of RJ Pennell, Photoimages. com*

The Spanish mission-inspired style house has an entry courtyard with a fountain, which provides an outdoor room and expands the living space. *Courtesy of Drew Hubbell*

Passive cooling features include an arched straw bale arcade built along the west side of the house, which minimizes solar heat gain in the summer and adds to the Mediterranean style. *Courtesy of Drew Hubbell*

A cooling tower with a fan and windows enhances the boulder's thermal mass effects. The tower cools in the summer by drawing out hot air and re-circulates warm air in the winter. *Courtesy of Drew Hubbell*

Exterior view of cooling tower and low water landscaping. *Courtesy of RJ Pennell, Photoimages. com*

The smooth side of the boulder serves as a wall in the master bedroom. All rooms enjoy natural light from upper windows in the cooling tower. *Courtesy of RJ Pennell, Photoimages. com*

An existing 11-foot granite boulder was left on site and incorporated into the design, maintaining a physical connection to the original landscape. Through its size and connection with the earth, the boulder moderates extreme swings in air temperature. *Courtesy of Drew Hubbell*

Surrounding the boulder is a moat with a pump and tubing system hooked up to the well and the solar hot water heater for further cooling and heating when necessary. A single wood-burning stove, which is rarely used, provides further heating. *Courtesy of RJ Pennell, Photoimages. com*

Hubbell & Hubbell used salvaged gothic arched mahogany doors and wood windows throughout the house. Interior walls are finished with earthen plaster. *Courtesy of Drew Hubbell*

The home's southern exposure features a large patio and in-ground swimming pool passively heated by the sun. *Courtesy of Drew Hubbell*

Massachusetts Geothermal House

Maryann Thompson Architects designed this 8,000 square-foot residence, in glass, steel, and wood, as a combination one and two-story house that steps gracefully into its meadow landscape. Occupying the space between the ground and the tree canopy, the residence provides an unfolding spatial experience, which repeatedly attempts to relate the interior spaces to the adjacent landscape. *Courtesy of Chuck Choi*

The house is conceived as a series of horizontal planes that terrace along the edge of a south-facing hill above a pond. The arrangement of the guest wing, main living spaces and bedroom wing, which wrap along the hill's crest, are a response to the topography, solar orientations, and views beyond. From the entry courtyard, the low profile of the house and selective openings through the facade allow for a playful hide and reveal of the landscape beyond without dominating the site. *Courtesy of Chuck Choi*

The house is organized on the site to take advantage of the daily path of the sun. The kitchen faces east while the living room and its terrace face west to take advantage of the setting sun. All rooms receive light on two sides. The combined living room, dining room, and kitchen area receives light on four sides through the use of a clerestory, enabling the sun to always be an ever-changing presence in the main body of the house. *Courtesy of Chuck Choi*

Large overhanging trellises and existing mature trees dapple and modulate intense summer sunlight, cooling the house's interior in summer. *Courtesy of Ioana Urma*

Selective openings in the north facade allow for a veiled reading of the landscape. Light pouring in through clerestory windows increases dependency on daylight vs. artificial light sources. *Courtesy of Ioana Urma*

The house is designed to tread lightly on the environment. The north facade is more insular while the south facade opens the house to the site and the sun. Attention has been paid to creating cross-ventilation through all the rooms. Large overhanging trellises modulate and dapple the intense summer western and southern sun at the living room and master bedrooms, while allowing in the winter sun. Both the heating and cooling systems are geothermal. *Courtesy of Stephen Lee*

Clerestory windows wrap the combined living/dining/kitchen area, illuminating the volume on four sides and providing an array of changing light conditions throughout the day and across the seasons. *Courtesy of Stephen Lee*

When one tugs at a single thing in nature he finds it attached to the rest of the world. –John Muir

5. REMODELED, REUSED, REFASHIONED

Green design is not just about preserving nature and conserving energy, it is also concerned with saving our resources – whether they be materials or buildings.

Our forebears reused materials. We all marvel at St. Peter's Basilica in Rome, but it was built from materials taken from The Coliseum, one of the greatest works of Roman architecture and engineering. New Englanders used to take rocks from old stonewalls to build new walls. Today, because of rising landfill costs, tighter recycling guidelines, and the growing trend toward ecologically sound building methods, home "deconstruction," as some call it, is becoming more popular.

Unfortunately, some 245,000 houses in the United States are razed each year, according to a 1996 Environmental Protection Agency report. This destruction generates nearly 20 million tons of debris. Some states, such as Massachusetts, have banned brick, concrete, metal, wood, and asphalt from landfills. Others require that homeowners pay deposits based on the size and type of project. To get the money back, they must show that 90 percent of the material generated has been reused or sent to a certified recycling or reuse center.

Renovating or refashioning an older building increases the financial return on the initial investment, allows us to preserve the energy used to make it originally, and prevents unnecessary disruption of a neighborhood. By remodeling, the building can remain in place, mellowing with time.

Whether the goal is to lower energy costs or enhance value, a new generation of consumers is "remodeling green." By utilizing alternative materials and construction methods, they're creating homes that improve the environment by using sustainable and recyclable resources and energy-efficient products.

Dana Point Remodel

Utilizing a variety of green techniques, Brion Jeannette refashioned the original 1960s ranch style home into a house with a Zen atmosphere. Dual-glazed low-E glass and fully operable glass walls infuse both natural light and ventilation and allow the peaceful water gardens and simple landscaping to blend seamlessly with the quiet and peaceful interiors. Sustainable building materials, including certified harvested renewable woods, are used throughout the house. Passive solar strategies are employed throughout the house. Operable skylights provide both interior natural day lighting as well as natural ventilation. Solar tubes are employed to provide diffused and bright daylight in a variety of interior spaces. *Courtesy of Eric Figge. com*

This water garden entry with random stepping pads is home to a variety of very happy koi and welcomes a maximum of natural light and every type of weather to be experienced from within. Long overhangs on all harsh exposures reduce heat gain and ease the blending of interior and exterior space, which can be enjoyed throughout the house. *Courtesy of Eric Figge. com*

Embodied Energy. One term that is often used in studying the green way of life is embodied energy, which refers to the energy required to extract and process the raw materials, manufacture the product, and transport the material and product from source to end use. Building materials with high embodied energy include asphalt, metals, glass and petroleum-based thermoplastics used as siding, flooring, insulation and vapor barriers. Building products with lower embodied energy include wood, wood and agricultural fiber, reused materials and many recycled content and byproduct-based products.

The Pacific Ocean is the centerpiece of this welcoming living room of this 3,600 square-foot home. High vaulted ceilings encased in certified harvested renewable woods extend through the house and provide a deep overhang that protects from the harsh southwest sun exposure. In winter, this same exposure provides heat gain through thermal massing. *Courtesy of Eric Figge. com*

Operable north-facing skylights infuse the open kitchen with plenty of natural light and ventilation. Solar panels are used for domestic hot water. The Lutron Homeworks Interactive lighting system allows for reduced lighting output and site-specific task lighting. Fluorescent task lighting allows for specific area lighting and further reduces energy consumption. High mass floor and counter materials provide additional heating and cooling retention. *Courtesy of Eric Figge. com*

Architect's Sustainable Design Residence

Ken Wilson, a founding principal of Envision and the architect owner of this house, demonstrates that a sensitive addition to a classic mid-century modern residence can be combined with an integrated sustainable design approach. In addition to enlarging his own house, he upgraded the existing builder-grade items such as hardware, windows, HVAC equipment, plumbing fixtures, appliances, and lighting and installed cedar siding over the existing T-111 plywood siding. The roof slopes to the front of the house so that rainwater runs off the roof and into a gravel-covered rainwater catchment area topped with Mexican river rocks for retaining water on site. © *Eric Lagnel*

Deciduous trees shade the house in warm seasons, and existing overhangs shade south-facing glass. The custom millwork credenza is made from wheatboard with FSC certified beech veneer. © *Eric Lagnel*

Increased insulation and natural cross-ventilation strategies combined with energy-efficient HVAC equipment, lighting, and appliances reduced total energy use by 6 percent, although the addition added 36 percent more space to the house. Ken used formaldehyde-free insulation with 25 percent recycled content throughout. A new high-albedo (white) membrane roof system reflects the roof heat. Installed over rigid foam insulation that is 1-1/2-inch thick, this system replaced the existing built-up roof. © *Eric Lagnel*

Wilson's design called for the installation of custom built-in millwork in the living, dining, kitchen, bathrooms, and master bedroom and new roll down shades to mitigate low winter sun angles and provide insulation. Floors were refinished, and new drywall replaced original walls clad in cheap paneling. Dining chairs were salvaged from another site and refurbished. © *Eric Lagnel*

All new kitchen appliances are Energy Star rated, including refrigerator, dishwasher, clothes washer, dryer, and ceiling fans. All light fixtures have CFLs or halogen PAR lamps (no incandescent A lamps). There is fluorescent under-cabinet lighting and a lamp in a classic George Nelson pendant light fixture. Custom millwork cabinets are made from wheatboard with caramelized solid bamboo plywood doors. Stainless steel countertop contains recycled content and can be recycled. © *Eric Lagnel*

Custom millwork cabinets in the master bathroom are made from wheatboard with caramelized solid bamboo plywood doors. Low flush toilets were installed, and recyclable copper piping was used in lieu of PVC for plumbing waste lines. © *Eric Lagnel*

To meet his goal of using eco-friendly materials and design strategies without compromising the original style of the house, Ken used brick from an old Baltimore warehouse that matched the original brick to wrap the original house. One hundred percent of electricity comes from wind energy through green energy credits, © *Eric Lagnel*

Storm Runoff. In some areas, excessive storm water run off is a problem. Green site design strategies include keeping as much storm water runoff on site as possible. Ken Wilson's gravel-filled trench holds the roof storm water on site until it can slowly soak into the soil in lieu of running down a downspout, down the hill and off into the street. He has filled the trench with gravel and topped it with Mexican river rocks to give it a Zen garden look. *Courtesy of Ken Wilson*

Green Makeover

The original 1940s house had two bedrooms and one bath in 1,350 square feet. Designed by Thompson & Naylor, the remodeled finished house has three bedrooms and two baths in 1,940 square feet. It also earned a 3-star Built Green Santa Barbara award. This image shows the new gable roof, new windows, with color integrated stucco, and 50-year roofing. *Courtesy of www. emilyhagopian. com*

The remodeled living room has a raised ceiling and bamboo flooring. Replacing the original fireplace, the south-facing French doors on the left allow passive solar heating in winter. An acacia wood countertop is visible at left. *Courtesy of www. emilyhagopian. com*

The new kitchen as seen from the former dining room area has formaldehyde-free cabinets, zero-VOC paint, raised acacia wood countertops, and LED lights, which are more efficient than halogen and incandescent lights and can last for 20 years. The aquasane water filtration system provides clean fresh water for the residents. *Courtesy of www. emilyhagopian. com*

In keeping with the principles of green architecture, the new acacia countertop was milled from the neighbor's tree, which was removed to enhance solar gain. *Courtesy of www. emilyhagopian. com*

The remodeled child's bedroom has bamboo flooring. *Courtesy of www. emilyhagopian. com*

Toothpick House

The farmhouse had burned down, but the barn and corncrib still stood. David Block AIA designed this energy-efficient sustainable residence on the site, inventing an exposed wood construction system to pay homage to the still standing barn and corncrib. All wood, both structural and for the siding and ceiling, is no-knot Douglas fir. The result is a 4,000 square-foot house that derives 75 percent of its needed winter heat from direct gain passive solar, with the rest coming from a geothermal heat pump, which utilizes a farm pond west of the house as its source of energy. Summer cooling is free because it relies on the cool water from the pond bottom. A wind machine, placed on top of the old windmill tower, generates domestic hot water.

This summer daytime south view shows the vast amount of glass, both straight and curved, the fir wood garage doors, and the unique wood structural system. The 1.5-inch square columns are spaced 1.5-inch apart and held together by 1/2-inch oak dowels. These are seen both on the exterior of the house and extending above the roof like delicate "toothpicks." *Photo by David Block AIA*

This summer nighttime view shows the openness of the interior and the southerly views, as well as the delicate columns that are both inside and outside the house. The use of wood on the interior helps create a warm and inviting glow to the night visitor. *Photo by King Au of Studio Au*

This summer daytime view also shows the south thermopane wall of the house, as well as the rounded forms that were used to soften the otherwise rigid structural system. The view to the west shows the beauty of the Iowa countryside. *Photo by David Block AIA*

This interior view from the foyer looks west across the dining room and into the living room. The kitchen is to the right, which is the center of the house – just as kitchens were in old Iowa farmhouses. The passive solar heat is stored in a 4-inch concrete slab below the black slate floor, with concrete being used at a minimum. The exposed structural system is clearly evident here, with every piece having a needed structural function. *Photo by David Block AIA*

This interior view from an upper walkway looks across the high ceiling of the dining room and the living room. The parts of the passive solar system are clearly evident here: the collector (south glass), the mass (slate and concrete floor), and the openness (convective loops). All pieces, even the handrails, are 1.5-inch pieces and always in groups of two or four. *Photo by King Au of Studio Au*

This interior view is from an upper walkway. It looks across the slatted floor walkway, through the south glass, and conveys the setting of the house, the corncrib, and foreground. The shadows and sun patterns in a direct gain passive solar house are extremely interesting, as they change constantly throughout the day. *Photo by King Au of Studio Au*

This image shows the "toothpick" structure, the wood joinery, and the dowels close-up. No nuts or bolts were utilized in the structure. *Photo by David Block AIA*

Selected for an Iowa American Institute of Architects Design Award, the day lit house is nestled within the trees surrounded by the constructed farm pond, barn, corncrib, and silo. A designed raft was constructed around an old tree stump. This pastoral setting shows the beauty of the Iowa countryside under the "big sky."*Photo by David Block AIA*

Newport Beach Home

Through an extensive remodel, Brion Jeannette gave this lovely home new life. The existing house had great bone structure and good solar orientation. Wherever possible, the remodel used the existing framing, adding sustainable building features. The landscape compliments the Zen environment with California native plant material. Long roof overhangs are employed to soften the use of natural day lighting and reduce solar heat gain. A Lutron Homeworks Interactive lighting system installed throughout the house reduced energy consumption. An active solar system heats domestic hot water, the pool, and spa. *Photography by David Heath ©Western Exposure*

Brion Jeannette designed an entry water garden on either side of the long exterior corridor, emphasizing an Asian theme including a meditation pagoda. A water feature cascades down the rock wall leading through the water garden to the front door. *Photography by David Heath ©Western Exposure*

The remodel opened the entire southwest exposure of the house to the exterior, bringing in the daylight to the home. In this temperate climate, the gentle cooling bay breezes provide a generous amount of natural ventilation throughout the house, circulating into the second story living spaces. Dual glazed low-E, bi-folding doors tuck clearly out of sight and enclose the space during inclement weather. *Photography by David Heath ©Western Exposure*

Large overhangs and pergolas reduce the solar heat gain and offer shelter from the sun for all year lounging on the bay view patio. Clean, gas burning flames dance around the exterior fireplace accented by fire rock spheres and gently take off the night chill. *Photography by David Heath ©Western Exposure*

The solar-heated horizon edge pool and elevated Japanese soaking spa compliment the bay view. *Photography by David Heath ©Western Exposure*

Previously, this dark office space required constant electrical lighting, but the remodel incorporated expansive walls of dual-glazed low-E glazing systems. Long roof overhangs protect the space from solar heat gain. *Photography by David Heath ©Western Exposure*

The roof deck offers protection from the sun. *Photography by David Heath ©Western Exposure*

Home as seen from the bay. *Photography by David Heath ©Western Exposure*

Responsible Stewards

Beautiful tree-lined streets and lush landscaping that invite summer evening strolling characterize this Redwood City neighborhood. The owners were very much interested in an environmentally sensitive solution, which would reconnect the house with the community, because the original structure turned its back on the street and had become a blight to the neighborhood.

Their desire to be responsible stewards of their little piece of land played an important role in the final outcome of the structure. Most of the environmentally responsible decisions were items that cannot even be seen, which is a great lesson in that your house does not have to look "different" in order to be good to Mother Earth. *Courtesy of Rossington Architecture*

Rossington Architecture took the original layout of the house and simply expanded on it and opened it up to the exterior to help promote more of an indoor-outdoor living experience. The house wraps around a cedar deck, which spills into the rear yard. This protected space is accessed on three sides from the family room, dining room, and bedroom wing hallway, allowing the exterior space to become an extension of the house. More than 75 percent of the non-roofed area is permeable, only a small amount of turf is used, and an efficient irrigation system has been implemented. *Courtesy of Rossington Architecture*

The deep overhang of the front porch provides a respite from the sun and connects the house to the neighborhood. Finely detailed horizontal rails help ground the house to its site. A base of cultured stone hides the fly ash-infused concrete foundations. The existing magnolia at the front of the lot and a large oak at the rear were carefully retained. *Courtesy of Rossington Architecture*

The porch is finely detailed with western red cedar railings and sun baffles. The deep overhang shades most of the house from the sun during the hottest parts of the day and provides a semi-private zone for the inhabitants to casually encounter passersby, helping connect the house and its inhabitants to its immediate environs. *Courtesy of Rossington Architecture*

Steel frames with aluminum screens help mitigate solar gain and glare, while operable awning windows allow the inhabitants to have windows open all day and night without compromising security. Energy-efficient, low-emissivity, dual-glazed windows help the thermal performance of the building while reducing harmful UV rays. *Courtesy of Rossington Architecture*

The entry is separated from the dining room by a bamboo screen, allowing views through and helping tie the interior to the exterior by creating a similar expression as is found on the porch rails and fences. *Courtesy of Rossington Architecture*

The kitchen with its Energy Star appliances is the hub of the house. The living room to the right has a series of clerestory windows for cross ventilation on hot days. Ceiling fans also help to efficiently cool the house and push heated air down during winter months. The floors are red oak, with water-based stain, and the walls are covered with low VOC paint. *Courtesy of Rossington Architecture*

The kitchen opens onto the dining room and the living room. A bamboo-clad pantry and powder room separate it from the family room. The bamboo is sustainably harvested, and the way it is laid up doesn't require edge banding. A large skylight in the kitchen and windows at counter height eliminate the need for the lights to be turned on during the day. *Courtesy of Rossington Architecture*

A large skylight and clerestory windows eliminates the need for lights in the master bath during the day. Glass tile and black granite slabs offset white counter-mounted bowls and field tile. *Courtesy of Rossington Architecture*

The outbuilding doubles as a garage and woodshop. The separate buildings help with sound and thermal insulation issues and help bring down the scale of the complex. Occupant health may also be adversely affected by car emissions leaking from the garage into the home, so separate structures deal with this potential hazard. *Courtesy of Rossington Architecture*

6. MULTI-UNIT HOUSING

Today, solar panels, tankless water heaters, and new insulation materials are becoming fixtures in apartments, condominiums, and new housing developments – not just custom built houses! Open courts or atria reduce the need for daytime lighting and increase natural ventilation. Whether it is an on-the-go lifestyle for the still young at heart, a multi-use development, or premier golf course living, we have many possibilities.

Adeline Street Urban Salvage

This Berkeley property was a 2 1/2-story, two-unit Victorian and an adjacent one-story retail building that Leger Wanaselja Architecture renovated in an ecologically sensitive manner. The completed work, a mixed-use property with two, ground-level commercial units and two residential units above, maintains and embellishes the character of the original house by using salvaged material and dramatically restructuring some of the spaces.

Completed in 2001, this remodel and addition won several awards including the national AIA's Top Ten Green Buildings. Green features include, high-volume fly ash concrete, 90-percent salvaged or FSC-certified sustainably harvested wood, blown-in cellulose insulation, new double pane wood windows, low and non toxic finishes, extensive use of salvaged materials, and a new urban-infill office space. For example, the firm lifted the existing residential building an entire story to add a second commercial unit at the ground floor. In the top unit, it opened four rooms together to create a large, sun-filled living space and put the bathroom in a former closet under the eaves. *Courtesy of Linda Svendsen*

Leger Wanaselja Architecture's design created a new roof deck and added windows to the west facade to take advantage of the sunshine and spectacular views in the upper unit. Mazda hatchback glass awnings and truck tailgate railings add humor to the project. *Courtesy of Ethan Kaplan Photography*

A warren of smaller rooms was opened up to create an airy yet compact living, dining, and kitchen area. Windows to the west take advantage of spectacular views and sunlight. The new double-pane low-E windows, combined with new blow- in cellulose insulation, dramatically improved the thermal comfort and energy performance of the building. *Courtesy of Ethan Kaplan Photography*

The different areas are subtly zoned by changes in ceiling height and lighting. Although the area for each use is small, they visually "borrow" from adjacent zones and as a result feel much larger. *Courtesy of Ethan Kaplan Photography*

Salvaged California Bay Laurel and recycled glass terrazzo make excellent countertops in this efficient open galley style kitchen. *Courtesy of Ethan Kaplan Photography*

Detail of Volvo hatchback railing. *Courtesy of Karl Wanaselja*

Beverly Skyline Co-Housing

A couple and the wife's sister planned to live in a co-housing arrangement that allowed separation of the couple and sister's personal spaces while sharing the public spaces. The house, designed by Barley & Pfeiffer, included offices for all three owners and a business in the lower level with its own entrance. Awarded the Austin Green Builder Program's Four Star Rating, the 4,350 square-foot house was selected for the 2001 AIA Homes Tour. © *Connie Moberly*

An established neighborhood lot at the crest of a steep hill offered breathtaking views yet faced into the hot Texas afternoon sun, which presented inspiration as well as obstacles! Barley & Pfeiffer's design made extensive use of shading trellises, awnings, and covered and screened porches so the residents could enjoy the views while being shielded from the Texas sun. © *Connie Moberly*

Since the bulk of energy costs in central Texas are spent on cooling the home, the focus of Barley & Pfeiffer's energy reduction strategy was to reduce heat gain. The metal roof contains a self-venting radiant barrier system, which keeps attic temperatures 40 to 50 degrees cooler than a typical attic in the area! Insulation board installed under the upstairs ceiling provides a thermal break between the finished ceiling and the roof structure. The windows and oversized roof overhangs throughout the home are designed and sized to provide summer shading, yet allow for ample natural lighting and natural winter heating from the sun. All windows had sun angle calculations performed on them. © *Connie Moberly*

The exterior wall sheathing is thoroughly wrapped in a special heavy-duty building wrap installed in such a way to keep moisture out of the walls. © *Connie Moberly*

The screened porch is strategically placed to capture breezes that naturally rise up from the drop off to the west. The windows are placed and arranged to provide for good cross ventilation, which, when coupled with high windows, helps exhaust hot air by way of "thermal siphons." © *Connie Moberly*

The exterior stone is locally quarried, reducing the "embodied energy" content of this home. The client and the landscape designer made extensive use of xeriscaping. Greywater is diverted for future use in landscaping needs. © *Connie Moberly*

The house used many green building materials, including Termi-mesh non-toxic termite treatment coupled with application of non-toxic Timbor insecticide in wall cavities prior to sheetrock installation; low VOC interior paint; wet blown cellulose insulation (formaldehyde-free); and bamboo, ceramic and tile floors. © *Connie Moberly*

The solar heating system consists of four 4 x 6 foot roof-mounted solar collectors and a 120 gallon stainless steel storage tank, located adjacent to the basement water heater. The solar storage tank supplies preheated water to both water heaters. The 17 SEER water-cooled, zoned air conditioning uses a small cooling tower, which employs evaporative cooling to improve efficiency. The air handlers are hydronic units. The duct system is constructed of sealed sheet metal, maximizing even airflow throughout the house to diminish the chance of some rooms being warmer, or cooler, than others. © *Connie Moberly*

2020 Green Dream

The front of this renovated three-flat building, built in 1876, reflects the form, massing, and scale of its 130 year-old Chicago neighbors. Thanks to a careful renovation by Wolbrink Architects, the character and style of this 5,900 square-foot building have survived along with the actual structure, but now it is an award-winning LEED-registered three flat, which won Mayor Dailey's 2006 Greenworks Award for Market Transformation because of its sustainable green building principles, materials, and a thoughtful site strategy. This high density urban infill is the First Energy Star Rated three flat in Chicago! Environmentally sound design solutions employed in the 2020 Green Dream include the use of low VOC finishes, regionally sourced and recycled content building materials, water-saving fixtures, green roofs, Energy Star appliances, and efficient mechanical systems that do not deplete the ozone. The result is a 58-percent reduction in energy use. *Courtesy of Dan Monteros/DRFP*

Regionally Sourced Materials. Sustainable design minimizes importation of goods and energy and works in harmony with the natural features and resources surrounding the proposed site. It uses renewable indigenous building materials where feasible. The wood of this house and the framing materials come from a nearby island in Glacier Bay, Alaska. Consequently, less energy is used to transport the material. *Courtesy of Sean Neilsen*

The brilliant natural light shining through low-E windows frames a striking hearth of locally quarried stone and brick. To maximize indoor air quality, no VOC primer and paint were used on interior finishes. *Courtesy of Dan Monteros/DRFP*

An electrifying CFL lighting scheme is used in the dining/living area to supplement the natural light. Energy efficient multi-light designer fixtures and cove lighting are used throughout. *Courtesy of Dan Monteros/DRFP*

The stair is constructed from magnificent locally harvested FSC (Forest Stewardship Council) certified maple stair and flooring with low VOC varnish finish. *Courtesy of Dan Monteros/DRFP*

Eye-catching locally harvested FSC certified maple and birdseye maple veneer and wheat board cabinets contain no urea-formaldehyde resins and accommodate the recycling center. *Courtesy of Dan Monteros/DRFP*

Luxurious bathrooms become a focal point for water and energy efficiency strategies featuring dual flush toilets and water-saving fixtures, Energy Star fans, and maximum natural lighting. The locally quarried limestone countertops, porcelain tiles, and water fixtures minimize fossil fuel usage from material transportation. *Courtesy of Dan Monteros/DRFP*

The lovely fountain in the captured rainwater pond provides soothing noise and visual peace for all who live nearby. The building also offers backlit, floating entry steps, which eliminate light trespass. Private outdoor spaces provide daily enjoyment of historic elm tree and skyline view. *Courtesy of Dan Monteros/DRFP*

Innovative, highly insulated aluminum panels on the exterior walls create an airtight efficient envelope. The extensive green roof fights urban heat island effect, creates a natural habitat, retains rainwater, and extends the roof life. Requiring no maintenance, it is an effective storm water management tool for highly developed urban areas. *Courtesy of Dan Monteros/DRFP*

The Dwight Way

Leger Wanaselja Architecture restored the original building and added a new building on the same site to create a nine-unit, mixed-use, urban infill project known as Dwight Way in the heart of Berkeley. Built originally as a corner grocery store with apartments above and a large side yard, the location had become one of the noisiest and busiest in the city. By restoring the existing building and adding a new one in an environmentally sensitive way, their work transforms this site into a highly acclaimed green showcase. *Courtesy of Cesar Rubio Photography*

Salvaged car parts and street signs enliven the facades of the project, drawing viewers in to discover other green features such as passive solar design, onsite rainwater management, and resource-efficient material use. *Courtesy of Karl Wanaselja*

Many green components can be seen in this interior of one of the new units. Visible are plaster walls with no paint, salvaged wood counters and sill, and FSC-certified sustainably harvested hardwood, seconds' light fixture, and hi-volume fly ash concrete with natural pigment finishes. The passive solar design with big south windows and doors, extra thick walls with recycled blown-in cellulose newspaper, and FSC-certified sustainably harvested 2 x 6 framing lumber is invisible. These two-bedroom units average less than 800 square feet, but careful planning and high ceilings create a gracious open feeling. *Courtesy of Cesar Rubio Photography*

This detail of this unit shows environmentally friendly wool carpet, FSC-certified sustainably harvested hardwood stairs, and artfully stained and scored high-volume fly ash concrete floor. The beautiful concrete finishes obviate the need to cover them with carpet. *Courtesy of Karl Wanaselja*

Over three tons of old street signs were used for siding and other elements on the two buildings. *Courtesy of Karl Wanaselja*

This remodeled unit in the existing building has carved salvaged columns and beams and Mazda hatchback glass, which make a fun and engaging railing. A new skylight adds daylight and extra ventilation. Other energy saving measures include replacement of all single pane windows with double pane low-E ones and addition of blown-in cellulose insulation. *Courtesy of Karl Wanaselja*

A generous courtyard between the two buildings provides bicycle parking and a quiet garden for community use. Salvaged brick and nontoxic, porous decomposed granite were used rather than asphalt in the parking area. The concrete paths, foundations and some finished floors are high-volume fly ash. Just this measure alone kept 31,000 pounds of carbon dioxide out of the atmosphere. *Courtesy of Cesar Rubio Photography*

Volkswagen headlights were repurposed as landscape lighting. The project achieved a 280-percent improvement in energy use in the existing building. The new building is almost twice as energy efficient as required by the state energy code. It has won several awards and been featured in a number of publications and television news stories. *Courtesy of Karl Wanaselja*

I say 'try.' If we never try, we shall never succeed. –President Abraham Lincoln

RESOURCES

Altius is a Toronto-based architectural firm that specializes in residential projects with a focus on sustainability. The firm's LEED-accredited professionals offer clean contemporary designs that emphasize craftsmanship and natural materials. Their award-winning projects are known for their sensitivity to site, thoughtful interiors, and innovative green design.

Altius's close attention to detail and client-driven design ethos produce intimate projects that are as unique as their owners. Its urban projects are engaging and contextual while their work in rustic Canadian regions, although bold in design, retires quietly into the landscape in true modernist tradition.

1 Atlantic Ave., Suite 120, Toronto, Ontario, Canada, M6K 3E7
Phone: 416.516.7772
Email; graham@altius. net
Web: www. altius. net

Since 1966, **BSB Design** has quietly earned a national reputation in residential architecture and community planning. The firm currently operates 15 regional offices coast to coast. A winner of hundreds of awards and honors, BSB Design has been the only architecture firm selected to design *The New American Home®* on three separate occasions.

Ed Binkley, AIA, National Design Director and partner of BSB Design, was the lead designer on the homes presented in this book. Mr. Binkley directs BSB Design's national initiative to introduce innovative and affordable green design concepts to homebuilders across the country. Soon, the firm will employ at least one LEED certified professional in each of its 15 regional offices, solidifying BSB Design's commitment to green building and affordable/workforce housing options.

Orlando Office: 261 Plaza Drive, Suite D, Oviedo, FL 32765
Phone: 407.359.4030
Email: ebinkley@bsbdesign. com

Corporate Office: 1601 West Lakes Parkway, Suite 200, West Des Moines, IA 50266
Phone: 515.273.3020
Email: info@bsbdesign. com

Steve Badanes and Jim Adamson are part of a loose-knit group of designer-builders, known as **Jersey Devil**, who have created projects that critique conventional practice, both the process of making architecture and the accepted definitions of architecture itself. Their architecture shows a concern for craft and detail, an attention to the expressiveness of the construction materials, and a strong environmental consciousness. All the members of Jersey Devil teach at the Yestermorrow Design/Build School in Warren, Vermont.

Steve Badanes also directs the Neighborhood Design/Build Studio at the University of Washington in Seattle.

Steve Badanes/Jersey Devil, Box 355720, UW, Seattle WA 98195
Phone: 206.543.7144
Email: Sbadanes@u. washington. edu
        designbuild@yestermorrow. org
Web: www. jerseydevildesigndesignbuild. com

Barley & Pfeiffer Architects are recognized nationally for their pioneering use of environmentally responsive building design and construction techniques. Their work includes healthful low toxicity environments in medical facilities and private homes, energy-conserving design and construction, and rainwater harvesting for residential and commercial use. The firm's award-winning projects have been featured nationally in the media.

1800 West Sixth St., Austin, TX 78703
Phone: 512.476.8580
Email: info@barleypfeiffer. com
Web: www. barleypfeiffer. com

Located in Westport, CT, **Barry Katz Homebuilding, Inc.** is a small volume design-build firm known for creating one-of-a-kind residences that reflect New England's rich architectural heritage. The firm's philosophy is to produce homes that are designed and constructed in a sustainable manner. These homes capture the style and grace of an earlier era while incorporating the comfort and technology that today's homeowners expect. Barry Katz is a certified LEED AP.

Westport , CT
Phone: 203.454.2941
Email: bk@katzhome. com
Web: www. katzhome. com

David A. Block AIA began his work 31 years ago with the intent to design energy-efficient houses, be highly respectful of place and client, and do work that is aesthetically as well as technically unique and exciting. He has designed and constructed 33 houses, nearly all of them passive solar and sustainable. In addition, he has been a Professor of Architecture at Iowa State University for even longer, teaching what he practices as well as benefiting from his students.

4618 Westbend Dr., Ames, IA 50014
Phone: 515.292.1645
Email: dablock@qwest. net

From their light-filled office in San Francisco's vibrant Mission District, **Boor Bridges Architecture** combines the art and functionality of design to help people live, learn, and work in beautiful, sustainable places. Since 1992, they have designed a diverse range of public and private buildings, houses, interiors, and gardens. They refer to their work as humanist modernism – an architectural philosophy based on daylight-driven spatiality, elegant and minimal materials, and energy-efficient, technical sophistication. One of the two principals works closely with clients throughout the project, creating leadership continuity.

1686 15th St., San Francisco, CA 94103
Phone: 415.241.7160
Email: studio@boorbridges. com
Web: www. boorbridges. com

Brion Jeannette Architecture began in 1974 with a design philosophy focused on green architecture. A guiding force behind the creation of Title 24 energy codes for the State of California, Brion Jeannette's vision for conservation in design strategies stretches between total independence from public utilities to reduced energy consumption. The firm has spent 30+ years incorporating healthy building products, implementing passive and active solar strategies, and employing these techniques, generally without visible notice. "A building does not have to look different or cost more to be energy efficient. Respecting the environment, and designing to take advantage of all available passive strategies for heating, cooling, lighting, and ventilation just takes knowledge." Projects range in scope from 2,500 square-foot beach cottages to palaces around the world.

470 Old Newport Blvd., Newport Beach, CA 92663
Phone: 949.645.5854
Email: email@customarchitecture. com
Web: www. customarchitecture. com

Tom Brown is a LEED-accredited professional and a registered architect specializing in high-performance, environmentally responsible design. His Mead Wildlife Area DNR Headquarters & Education Center project received the 2006 Sustainability & Energy Efficiency (SE2) Award of Excellence, the highest honor for a green building in Wisconsin, the 2006 Wisconsin Governor's Award for Excellence in Sustainable Design and Construction, and the 2006 Award of Honor from the National Association of Conservation Engineers. The National Association of Home Builders Research Center selected another Brown project as the most Innovative/Advanced residence in a cold climate region in the U. S.

Tom is a founding member of the Energy & Environmental Building Association, the Wisconsin Green Building Alliance, and the Midwest Renewable Energy Association. A frequent presenter at local, regional, and national energy and sustainable building conferences, Tom teaches an environmental design course at UW-Stevens Point.

1052 Main St., Stevens Point, WI 54481
Phones: 715.341.9596; 888.416.1419
Email: tbjs@coredcs. com
Web: www. tombrownarchitect. com

Carter+Burton Architecture P. L. C. is a small Virginia architecture firm that specializes in a few good projects per year. Located in Berryville, a small town one hour west of Washington, D. C., its architects love to design and work within a wide range of budgets. The firm's focus is on qual-ity, craftsmanship, and innovation. It tries to promote passive solar techniques and eco-friendly building materials.

11 W. Main St., Berryville, VA 22611
Phone: 540.955.1644
Email: jim@carterburton. com
Web: www. carterburton. com

Matthew Coates, AIA LEED AP, founded **Coates Design, Inc.**, Seattle, in 2004. An award-winning architect, Matthew is forward thinking, focusing on where architecture and sustainable designs are heading, and uses technology to promote the most versatile use of energy and materials. The recipient of numerous honors and awards, Coates' work has been published in respected national publications, including *The Wall Street Journal, DWELL,* and *The New York Times.*

PO Box 11654, Bainbridge Island, WA 98110
Phone: 206.780.0876
Web: www. coatesdesign. com

Ken Wilson is the founding principal of **Envision**, a multidisciplinary design firm with a focus on environmental responsibility. Envision's work includes a variety of project types in the areas of architecture, interiors, and product design. The firm has received over 60 national and local awards since opening in the spring of 1999. All of Envision's design staff are LEED accredited professionals.

Ken received a Presidential Commendation in 2005 for his work in promoting environmentally responsible design and has been active in the development of the LEED Rating System serving on the U.S. Green Building Council's LEED Commercial Interiors and LEED Core & Shell National Core Committees. In 2005, Ken was the recipient of the *Contract* magazine's Designer of the Year Award and was included in *Metropolitan Home* magazine's prestigious "Design 100." Ken's work with Envision has been exhibited at the National Building Museum and has been published in numerous national design journals

1211 Connecticut Ave., NW, Suite 250, Washington, DC 20036
Phone: 202.775.9000
Email: kwilson@envisionsite. com
Web: www. envisionsite. com

A registered architect in the States of Connecticut, Massachusetts, Vermont, and New York, **George Fellner** is a member of the Connecticut Chapter of the American Institute of Architects and is certified by the National Council of Architectural Registration Boards. A primary focus for his work involves sustainable design strategies. As Co-Chairman of the Connecticut AIA Committee on the Environment, he is responsible for organizing programs and seminars related to sustainability, including alternative technologies and materials. He has presented many programs on geothermal systems. He was also a speaker at the AIS 2008 National Convention on Geothermal Systems.

415 Killingworth Rd., Higganum, CT 06441
Phone: 860.345.7558
Email: fellnerarchitects@sbcglobal. net
Web: www. fellnerarchitects. com

Gary Graham, FAIA, is an Adjunct Professor of Architecture at Roger Williams University School of Architecture, Art, and Historic Preservation, and a principal and co-founder of the Boston-based architectural firm: **Graham/Meus Inc. Architects.** An architect, planner, and facilitator, his solutions evolve from the functional, cultural, and physical context of each unique situation. His institutional, residential, and commercial projects have received state, regional, and national design awards and been the subject of articles in national publications. He has had a career-long interest in the effects of climate and environment on architecture, since his experience as a Peace Corps Volunteer in Colombia, South America.

6 Edgerly Place, Boston, MA 02116
Phone: 617.423.9399 x215

1289 Anthony Rd., Portsmouth, RI 02871
Phone: 401.293.0880
Email: ggraham@graham-meus. com
Web: www. Graham-Meus. com

Doug Graybeal, AIA, founded **Graybeal Architects, LLC,** a unique architectural firm focusing on environmentally friendly design in 2004. He prides himself on "design with a conscience." Through his innovative design process, individualized client goals inspire distinctive architecture that is both creative and functional while reducing impacts on the environment and our health. Graybeal Architects, LLC, provides architectural services from conceptual design through construction documents and including construction observation services.

Graybeal strives to use his 30 years of professional experience to create efficient architecture that is in harmony with its surroundings. He has lectured on energy-efficient design; his work has received many awards; and he continues to seek new avenues to improve the green design and building process.

188 Sunset Lane, Carbondale, CO 81623
Phone: 970.704.1188
Email: doug@graybealarchitects. com
Web: www. graybealarchitects. com

Hays + Ewing Design Studio (HEDS) is a full-service architecture and planning firm recently formed by architects Christopher Hays and Allison Ewing. Hays + Ewing have over 40 years of combined experience in designing award-winning commercial, cultural, residential, institutional, and planning projects. Firm co-founders, Christopher Hays and Allison Ewing, both formerly Design Partners at William McDonough + Partners and U. S. Green Building Council LEED-accredited professionals, bring expertise in incorporating aesthetic and ecological considerations in a range of building scales and types in projects located around the globe. They believe *good design merges beautiful solutions with ecological integrity* and seek to achieve this goal in all their projects.

Hays + Ewing's expertise in environmental building design includes the full range of environmental considerations: site design, water conservation, recycled, reclaimed and renewable material selection and sourcing, energy conservation, carbon neutral strategies, and indoor environmental quality. They incorporated these strategies in projects with clients such as Nike, IBM, Oberlin College, Ocean Conservancy, Museum of Life and the Environment, and many private residences.

609 East Market Street, Suite 203, Charlottesville, VA 22902
Phone: 434.979.3222
Email: aewing@hays-ewing. com
Web: www. hays-ewing. com

Since 1982, William Hoffman of **Hoffman Architecture** has pursed a creative private practice in Fort Lauderdale, Florida. Commissions have included residential, commercial, and interior, detail-oriented projects. Both museum and gallery exhibitions have featured his furniture, lighting fixtures, and in-house generated prototypes. Awards and publications have acknowledged the merit of his designs. His residential projects are environmentally friendly, site-specific designs, employing green and energy efficient techniques.

4070 NE 15th Terrace, Fort Lauderdale, FL 33334
Phone: 954.561.1642
Web: hoffarch@bellsouth. net

Holzman Moss Architecture is a national architectural practice with a 40-year legacy of making memorable spaces. Buildings that welcome public use are the mainstay of its practice. Its design methods originate with individual initiatives. Ideas advance through visualization, dialogue, and inquiry, surpassing client aspirations to extend and enrich the built environment. Its expertise includes governmental and municipal buildings, as well as master planning and design for a wide range of facilities for higher education.

214 West 29th St. Tower, 17th Fl., New York, NY 10001
Phone: 212.465.0808 x236
Email: jblum@holzmanmoss. com
Web: www. holzmanmoss. com

Hubbell & Hubbell, a collaborative firm of artists and architects, creates forms based on the beauty of nature and ecologically sound building practices. The team develops places that heal the soul and renew the spirit through organic design solutions. Their work is unique because of its sensitivity to the environment, innovative design, and detailing. The firm's diverse experience ranges from designing private residences using energy- efficient materials to a boulder-shaped ecological center in Tecate, Mexico, to international public art projects like the Pacific Rim Parks in China, Russia, San Diego, and Mexico. Dedicated to sustainable design solutions, the Hubbell architecture studio is known for its pioneering straw bale work.

1970 Sixth Ave., San Diego, CA 92101
Phone: 619.231.0446
Email:info@hubbellandhubbell. com
Web: www. hubbellandhubbell. com

Michael McElhaney, AIA, joined the office of Robert Jackson Architects in Austin in 1988 and received his architectural license in 1991. After sixteen years of successful collaboration, they formed **Robert Jackson & Michael McElhaney Architects** in 2004. The firm strives to create a unique, site-specific design for each individual client, with an emphasis on environmental responsibility. Their list of accomplishments includes: five national and international design awards, including 2006 AIA/COTE Top Ten Green Project Award; 10 statewide design awards; and 21 local design awards, including two 5-star rated and one 3-star rated Green Building residences, along with a 2-star rated Green Building school.

1135 West 6th St., Suite 125, Austin, TX 78703
Phone: 512.472.5132
Email: mike@jacksonmcelhaney. com
Web: www. JacksonMcElhaney. com

The **Jersey Devil** is a loose-knit group of designer-builders. The members of Jersey Devil teach at the Yestermorrow Design/Build School in Warren, Vermont. See Steve Badanes for more information.

Email: designbuild@yestermorrow. org
Web: online. caup. washington. edu/courses/hswdesign-build

Kelley and Kelley has won many awards, including two of the seven awards presented by the 1998 East Bay Chapter of the American Institute of Architects in recognition of outstanding achievements in architectural design in Alameda, Contra Costa, Solano, and Napa counties.

Bruce and Colette Kelley have a background in naval architecture. They have designed custom and production sailboats, including a World Champion under the International Offshore Rule, as well as custom and production motor yachts. Their work has been published worldwide. Kelley and Kelley now design custom homes full time and have won numerous design awards for their residential design work.

2015 Delaware St., Berkeley, CA 94709
Phone: 510.548.1001
Email: kelleyandkelley@SBCGlobal. net

Linda Kiisk, AIA LEED AP, is committed to designing places that respect the natural features of the site. Through her earlier work with historic properties, she observed that many dwellings were inherently sustainable in the way that they used local materials and related to the conditions of the site. She draws on these same principles when designing new structures. While operating her design practice, Ms. Kiisk served as a professor for various disciplines related to architecture and was the Associate Director of the Institute for the Built Environment, a sustainability institute located in Colorado. In this role, she was the principal investigator for a federal grant to produce a satellite broadcast to train National Park Service members in sustainable practices. One of the videos she co-created won an International Telly Award. In 2004, she was awarded a Fulbright in Heritage Tourism and Sustainable Development and Design. Today, she maintains a design practice in Wyoming and works as the Associate Director of Facilities Planning for the University of Wyoming.

University of Wyoming, Laramie, WY 82071
Phone: 307.766.2408
Email: lkiisk@uwyo. edu

Leger Wanaselja Architecture is an award-winning architecture and general contracting firm with a specialty in ecological design. It creates architecture specific to its place, believing that, at its essence, a work of architecture is a functional work of art. The firm integrates programmatic requirements with the specific geography, sunlight, and weather patterns of a site so that projects emerge naturally from their surroundings. Where possible, they incorporate local materials and reuse existing materials, reinforcing the relationship of project to place. The firm has won many awards and been featured in many books, magazines, television stories, and newspapers.

Karl Wanaselja has been studying, teaching, and practicing architecture since 1978. His photography and architectural designs have been exhibited in galleries across the country. He has worked with concrete, wood, steel, adobe, and straw structural systems and has extensive experience in the use of salvaged materials. Cate Leger has focused on "green" architecture since she began her graduate studies at U. C. Berkeley in 1991. She lectures regularly in the Bay Area on the firm's work and ecological design and construction.

2320 McGee Avenue, Berkeley, CA 94703
Phone: 510.848.8901
Email: lwarc@pacbell. net
Web: www. greendwellings. com

Maryann Thompson, a member of Harvard University's Architecture faculty, founded **Maryann Thompson Architects** in 2000; prior to that she was a founding partner of Thompson and Rose Architects. She specializes in sustainable, regionally driven architecture that attempts to heighten a sense of its immediate site and landscape. Her architectural investigations revolve around such concerns as the creation of a rich and thoughtful edge between inside and outside, utilizing light as a material, and employing warm, natural materials in order to accentuate a sense of place. Thompson carries degrees in both architecture and landscape architecture, bringing to her practice an interdisciplinary approach where issues of site and landscape are central to design thinking.

Her work has been widely published in *Landscape Architecture Magazine*, *Insite*, *Art New England*, *Progressive Architecture*, *Architecture*, *Architectural Digest*, *Architectural Record*, *A+U*, and in various architectural books, including Norton's *A Guide to 250 Key Twentieth-Century American Buildings*, *40 Under 40*, and *Contemporary American Architects*. Her work has received numerous awards and honors, including two AIA National Honor and numerous AIA New England awards.

14 Hillside Ave., Cambridge, MA 02140
Phone: 617.491.4144
Email: maryann@maryannthompson. com
Web: www. maryannthompson. com

John McConnell is a principal of **McConnell + Partners Architects Inc.** in Boston. Founded in 1987, the firm specializes in residential and small-scale institutional and commercial design, as well as historically sensitive additions and renovation of older buildings. Prior to founding the firm, John worked for Boston architectural firms, chiefly Shepley Bulfinch Richardson & Abbott, where he was the chief designer for several projects including the renovation of the historic Old South Church at Boston's Copley Square.

McConnell has been adjunct professor of American Architectural history at Boston College since 1979, a lecturer in architectural history at the Harvard Graduate School of

Design, and architecture lecturer-in-residence for the Museum of Fine Arts, Boston. He is the author of *Courthouses of the Commonwealth: A History of Superior Courthouse Architecture in Massachusetts* (UMass Press, 1984) and major contributor to *Shingle Style Houses, Then and Now* (Schiffer Publishing, 2006).

164 Canal St., Boston, MA 02114
Phone: 617.482.7500
Email: mcwinchest@earthlink. net
Web: www: McConnellArchitects. com

Michael Heacock + Associates is a design and consulting firm specializing in high performance green buildings. Working with its clients, it creates regenerative buildings that produce more energy than they consume, grow their own food, process their own waste, and cool the planet. The firm strives to create living, breathing buildings with natural ventilation, daylight, water harvesting, wind turbines, and photovoltaic panels – buildings of beauty. The firm also provides LEED and sustainability consulting services on projects seeking high-performance goals and environmental sensitivity. Through LEED Lab, Inc., the firm is able to contribute expertise on a wide range of environmentally sensitive projects.

1591 B Stillwell Rd., San Francisco, CA 94129
11 Romaine, Santa Barbara, CA 93105
Phone: 415.845.5326
Email: mh@michaelheacock. com
Web: www. michaelheacock. com

An award-winning firm operating in Austin, Texas, **Miró Rivera Architects (MRA)** offers a diverse array of projects, including: urban and interior design, institutional, commercial, and residential architecture. Its design signature entails diversity to fit the individual client's vision, while stringing a common thread of innovation throughout each project. MRA's work is characterized by the innovative use of structural systems, materials, and finishes; its designs are dramatic, elegant, and highly original.

The firm's work has been exhibited and published nationally and internationally. It has received design awards given by the American Institute of Architects in New York City, New York State, and Texas and also been honored by the Chicago Athenaeum and by the American Institute of Steel Construction.

505 Powell St., Austin, TX 78703
Phone: 512.477.7016
Email: info@mirorivera. com
Web: www. mirrivera. com

A partnership between two long-established Colorado firms created **OZ Architecture** in 1989. This unique concept brought together staff with varied expertise and client bases, creating a firm with the talent, people-power, and experience in a broad range of project types, to set a new standard in design excellence and commitment to service. The firm is a member of the U. S. Green Building Council and has 30 LEED-accredited architects and design specialists on its 200 + staff. OZ Architecture has earned more than 100 design awards for a wide variety of projects. Many of these awards are from the American Institute of Architects. It is also recognized by

several publications as one of the major design firms in the United States.

3012 Huron St., Suite 100, Denver, CO 80202
Phone: 303.861.5704

1820 Folsom Boulder, CO 80302
Phone: 303.449.8900
Email: ahammett@ozarch. com
Web: www. ozarchtiecture. com

Perkins VonDeylen & Associates (PVA) is an Indianapolis-based architecture firm dedicated to creating unique and innovative projects that are sensitive and appropriate to their setting. Established in 2000, its primary goal has always been client satisfaction. It partners with its clients to reveal the optimum design solution and is known for its user-friendly approach to the collaborative design process. The firm believes that architecture is an art, a science, and a business, and, therefore, its joy, discipline, and livelihood. Its practice includes particular strengths in both residential and commercial architecture.

410 South College, Suite 100, Indianapolis, IN 46203-1021
Phone: 317.803.7900
Email: szabel@pvanda. com
Web: www. pvanda. com

Founded in 1999 by Phil Rossington, **Rossington Architecture** is a full-service architectural firm dedicated to excellence in design and project management. The firm has won numerous awards. Its work is focused on residential projects, including additions, new homes, multifamily housing, and mixed-use. Projects have also included a yoga studio, two rock-climbing gyms, and a corporate retreat in Shanghai, China. The work derives directly from its context, taking cues from existing conditions and carefully interpreting the needs of the clients and focusing on how they use the spaces they occupy. Detailing is kept purposefully clean, simple, and timeless.

Prior to starting the firm, Rossington spent ten years at Solomon Architecture and Urban Design. During his tenure, he was responsible for a variety of projects including single-family homes, affordable housing, luxury town homes in Hong Kong, a medical facility in San Rafael, and a passively cooled funeral chapel in Houston.

4529 18th St., San Francisco, CA 94114
Phone: 415.552.4900
Email: phil@rossingtonarchitecture. com
Web: www. rossingtonarchitecture. com

Shubin + Donaldson Architects (S+D) is a high-design architecture firm that specializes in developing livable environments. Headed by partners Russell Shubin, AIA, and Robin Donaldson, AIA, the firm tailors its projects—custom residential, office buildings and interiors, retail, hospitality, planning, and multi-family housing—with a refined sensitivity toward the land and context. S+D considers itself not just an architectural firm but a high tech creative company with a creative studio atmosphere where creative experimentation is encouraged. It maintains a pragmatic budget and schedule discipline necessary to effectively work with other businesses.

3834 Willat Ave., Culver City, CA 90232
Phone: 310.204.0688x101
Email: taylorpr@usa. net
Email: www. shubinanddonaldson. com

Lindy Small came to architecture after studying music, a discipline that was instrumental in her developing an acute awareness of proportion, rhythm, and balance. Her work demonstrates a strong commitment to detail, quality, and design integrity. Her projects, rigorous in spatial relationships, material logic, and precision detailing, are responsive to her client's needs and desires and to the pleasure of making architecture.

95 Linden St., No.10, Oakland, CA 94607
Phone: 510.251.1066
Email: Lindy@LindySmallArchitecture. com
Web: LindySmallArchitecture. com

David V. Hartke, AIA, MBA, LEED AP, is a registered architect who holds a Masters Degree in Business Administration and is a LEED-accredited professional. Hartke was previously a NARI-certified builder and co-founded BrightRooms, Inc., a building company specializing in efficient home design and construction. Currently, he is a principal of **Stampfl Hartke Associates, LLC**, an architecture and engineering firm located in Holicong, Pennsylvania. Dave co-chairs at the Keystone Green Building Initiative (KGBI) for the Home Builders Association (HBA) of Bucks and Montgomery Counties. He is also a lead instructor for Bucks County Community College's "Substantial Building Advisor Program (SBA)".

2525 Holicong Rd., P.O. Box 667, Holicong, PA 18928
Phone: 215.794.1925 x222
Email: dhartke@stampflhartke. com
Web: www. stampflhartke. com

Edvin Karl Stromsten says about Project GreenHouse, "A great many traditional principles and contemporary technologies contribute to the design of a house. I want to emphasize that there is no single fact that is most important to the principles, but that it is the judicious combination of many factors that need to be molded into an integrated design. This in itself is a basic principle of architecture. "
Stromsten has offices in New York and East Hampton. His projects include large-scale urban renewal and rebuilding, institution, commercial, and residential work. He has taught at various schools, including The Cooper Union, the New School, City College, and New York Institute of Technology in New York, and the University of California in Berkeley. His focus now is to educate others about building green.

26 West 26 St., New York, NY 10010
Phone: 917.407.5103
Email: Edvinks@optonline. net

Specializing in both custom residential and commercial architecture, **Ross L. Tedter** has been a registered architect in Texas since 1982 and nationally certified by NCARB since 1988. A graduate of the University of Texas School of Architecture, he has over 31 years of architectural experience in all phases of service from schematic design through construction administration, covering a wide range of project types and

sizes, primarily in design and production. A strong believer in helping solve global environmental problems with exemplary local solutions, Tedter is a member of the Austin Energy Green Building Program and the Texas Solar Energy Society, where he offers considerable knowledge and interest in energy conscious design and sustainability.

1703 Treadwell St., Austin, TX 78704
Phone: 512.916.4241
Email: tedter@autin. rr. com

Thompson-Naylor Architects is an award-winning firm that practices "Socially and Environmentally Responsible Architecture and Planning." The firm has designed many sustainable residential and institutional projects; in 2001 it received the "Green Award" as an exemplary environmental business. In 2005, it received a "Flex Your Power" Honorable Mention from Southern California Edison for outstanding achievements in energy efficiency in education and leadership. Mr. Thompson has served on the County Board of Architectural Review, the Board of Directors of the Community Environmental Council, and The Sustainability Project, and he was founding president of the Green Building Alliance. He is a LEED- accredited professional and has taught and lectured extensively on design, sustainability, and green building.

900 Philinda Ave., Santa Barbara, CA 93103
Phone: 805.966.9807
Email: tna@thompsonnaylor. com
Web: www. thompsonnaylor. com

Translation of Space is an architectural collaborative made up of architects, interior designers, landscape designers, developers, and real estate professionals. Its goal is to promote contemporary, sustainable design that directly reflects the needs of its clients, and its architecture is an experiment in the marriage of these two progressive notions that go together so well. Andrew T. Mangan founded the firm in 2004.
The firm believes that good design starts with sustainability, and progressive architecture can be a vehicle for change. It understands that it is a privilege to take part in how its clients live day to day by taking that trust and translating space into beautiful, ecologically sensitive, contemporary buildings.

P. O. Box 2035, Venice, CA 90294
Phone: 310.383.8840
Email: andrew@tos-arc. com
Web: www. tos-arc. com

A full service studio founded in 2001, **VaST**'s work has been called modern, contemporary, and eclectic. The Bauhaus school, modernism, prairie style, and the Case Study Program inspire the studio's aesthetic. Although the firm doesn't believe in creating a false sense of history, it does enjoy the challenge of working on projects in established neighborhoods and imbuing them with contemporary elements that harmonize with the surrounding architecture. Its ultimate goal is to create an environment that functions well, looks beautiful, and uses resources wisely. Its objective is to design the most appropriate, stylish, and energy-efficient project for the budget. Its principals are LEED-accredited and green building.

2020 20TH St., Boulder, CO 80302

Phone: 303.442.3700
Email: brandy@VaSTarchitecture. com
Web: www. vast2020. com

Wolbrink Architects Chartered is synonymous with sustainable design strategies. A Green Design and Design Build firm, it attained its eco-sensitive design approach through the integration of environmental, social, and economic concerns into the design and construction of beautiful buildings. It believes that everyone on earth, now and in the future, benefits from high value buildings that are healthier for occupants and the environment and use fewer resources and that its expertise in new construction or renovation will generate a sound return on investment for years to come. It designs a future with a conscientious mind towards sustainable planning, materials, and construction techniques.

2018 W. Rice St., Chicago , IL 60622
Phone: 773.276.7026
Email: US@WolbrinkArchitects. com
Web: www. WolbrinkArchitects. com

David Wright has lived and practiced in Santa Fe, New Mexico , The Sea Ranch and Nevada City, California, designing over 500 passive solar and alternative construction buildings, both residential and commercial/institutional. He believes in designing structures that use the best suited organic materials and buildings and that naturally heat and cool themselves and use a minimum of offsite energy. To Wright, combining modern systems such as structural insulated panels with natural materials is a fascinating challenge. He has designed structures using wood, adobe, rammed earth, straw, rock, concrete masonry, and earth masonry as well as recycled materials. Today, the focus of his work is the innovative integration of advanced building materials along with passive solar and solar electric technologies into mainstream architectural environmental design. Nationally certified as an architect, he is licensed to practice in several states and can work throughout the United States as well as overseas.

Wright has written two books on passive solar architecture, *Natural Solar Architecture: A Passive Primer* and *Passive Solar Architecture: Logic & Beauty.* He has been published in many periodicals and books. including *Sunset Magazine, The Wall St. Journal, Architecture Magazine, Better Homes and Gardens, National Geographic,* and many others. He has also received design awards and recognition by many organizations and lectured throughout the United States and Europe. His work has been exhibited at several international exhibits as well as the Smithsonian Institute.

563-B Idaho Maryland Rd., Grass Valley, CA 95945
Phone: 530.477.5057
Email: dwright@netshel. net
Web: www. dwrightaia. com

OTHERS

Sean Neilsen and his wife Janet live in Gustavus, Alaska, along the southern boundary of Glacier Bay National Park. She works as a humpback whale biologist for Glacier Bay and volunteers as an Emergency Medical Responder (ETT) for the local fire department. Neilson is a professional photographer (www. seanneilson. com) who also works as a naturalist/guide. He spends a good deal of time on protein patrol harvesting, deer, moose, salmon, halibut, crab, shrimp, etc.

INDEX